Making ADHD a Gift

Teaching Superman How to Fly

Robert Evert Cimera

A SCARECROWEDUC.

The Scarecrow Pr
Lanham, Maryland, ;
2002

A SCARECROWEDUCATION BOOK

Published in the United States of America
by Scarecrow Press, Inc.
A Member of the Rowman & Littlefield Publishing Group
4720 Boston Way, Lanham, Maryland 20706
www.scarecrowpress.com

PO Box 317
Oxford
OX2 9RU, UK

British Library Cataloguing in Publication Information Available

Library of Congress Cataloging-in-Publication Data

Cimera, Robert E.
    Making ADHD a gift : teaching Superman how to fly / Robert E. Cimera.
        p. cm.
    "A Scarecrow Education book."
    Includes bibliographical references (p.).
    ISBN 0-8108-4319-6 (alk. paper)—ISBN 0-8108-4318-8 (pbk. : alk. paper)
    1. Attention-deficit-disordered children—Education—United States. 2. Attention-deficit
hyperactivity disorder. I. Title.

LC4713.4 .C56 2002
371.93—dc21
                                                                        2002021201

♾™ The paper used in this publication meets the minimum requirements of American
National Standard for Information Sciences—Permanence of Paper for Printed Library
Materials, ANSI/NISO Z39.48-1992.
Manufactured in the United States of America.

I would like to dedicate this book to those lifeforms who have had faith in my abilities and have overlooked my many oddities.

I would particularly like to thank the following (in no particular order): Nixon, Dante, Truman, Becky, Frank, Janis, Daizey, the wonderful people at the University of Illinois, CHADD, and Scarecrow Press, as well as Agnew.

Contents

Preface

Attention deficit hyperactivity disorders (ADHD) have received a great deal of consideration over the past decade, perhaps more than any other disability. Unfortunately, most of the clinical research and popular media have emphasized the need to repress ADHD symptoms such as hyperactivity, inattention, and impulsivity. As a result, parents and teachers frequently find themselves attempting to force children with ADHD to sit still or pay attention. These are battles that parents and teachers need not fight and will often lose.

ADHD is not a "disability." ADHD is a gift. Who among us would not want to have more energy or be more creative? Yet many professionals and parents rely on medications and punishments to make their children more "normal."

The purpose of this text is to give practical strategies to help individuals with ADHD utilize their natural abilities—in essence, to turn ADHD into a "super-ability." Because most individuals with ADHD are diagnosed during their school years, the term "students" is used throughout the following pages. However, most of the strategies presented here can be used both at home and at school.

As you read this text, please keep in mind that there is no "silver bullet" or "cure-all." What works for one student may not work with another. However, by focusing on the individual strengths that all students have, far more can be accomplished than by constantly trying to make them like their non-ADHD peers.

Making ADHD a Gift: Teaching Superman How to Fly is written for parents of children with ADHD and for teachers whose students have been diagnosed or students whose symptoms may resemble (although not yet diagnosed) ADHD. It is not my intention, however, to limit this book to only those readers. Employers, coworkers, other family members, social agencies, and anyone who is involved with other individuals who may have ADHD will find helpful strategies in this book.

CHAPTER 1

An Overview of Attention Deficit Hyperactivity Disorders

CHAPTER OBJECTIVES

This chapter answers the following questions:

1. What are "attention deficit hyperactivity disorders"?
2. What causes attention deficit hyperactivity disorders?
3. How are attention deficit hyperactivity disorders diagnosed?
4. How are attention deficit hyperactivity disorders treated?
5. What other conditions are associated with attention deficit hyperactivity disorders?
6. What are the primary characteristics of attention deficit hyperactivity disorders?

CASE STUDY: MARK

Mark is a twelve-year-old student in my class who displays several inappropriate behaviors. For instance, he shouts out answers if I do not call on him right away. Further, despite a warning every fifteen minutes or so, he walks around the classroom or talks when he should be working quietly at his desk. Finally, he has a tendency to bother other students, especially the girls who sit near him. Specifically, he pokes them with his pencil, makes inappropriate comments, or passes them notes or funny drawings.

It isn't that Mark is a bad kid; he isn't. In fact, he is very bright and can be quite charming. But lately, he doesn't seem to be paying much attention in class. Additionally, two to three times a week, he says that he "forgot" his assignments or books at home. Consequently, his grades are beginning to slip from a B+ average to slightly below a C.

I have tried punishing him with detentions, rewarding his appropriate behavior with praise, sending notes home to his parents, and counseling him during my free periods, but nothing seems to be working. I am at a loss. I have no idea how to reach him.

Case Study Questions

1. Do you think that Mark has an attention deficit disorder? Explain.
2. How would you determine if Mark's difficulties were caused by an attention deficit disorder?
3. What other conditions could explain Mark's behaviors?
4. If Mark has an attention deficit disorder, what type would he have?
5. How would you help Mark's teacher?

INTRODUCTION

Although estimates of its prevalence vary widely from study to study, approximately 3 to 5 percent of all children in the United States have an attention deficit disorder (American Psychiatric Association 1994). With this in mind, it is no wonder conditions such as attention deficit hyperactivity disorder (ADHD) make educators very concerned and more than a bit apprehensive. As figure 1.1 indicates, it is one of the most prevalent conditions that teachers will encounter.

Imagine that you are a regular educator and that it is your first day teaching. You open the door to your classroom, lesson plans in hand, only to see that most of your twenty-five students are sitting quietly at

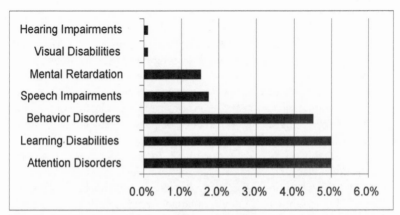

Figure 1.1 *Percent of Students with Various Disabilities*
Source: Deutsch, Smith, and Luckasson (1995); Thomas (1996)

their desks, waiting for you to begin the day. One or two students, however, are running around screaming, climbing on the bookshelves, or throwing things across the room. Meanwhile, a couple of other children are staring off into space. Further, no matter how hard you try, you just can't seem to get either of these groups to pay attention to you or their schoolwork.

What you just imagined is an exaggeration of the day-to-day reality of most regular educators. Most teachers have gone to college and have received their degrees in specific subjects or areas of concentration, such as history or early childhood. They do not have strong backgrounds in how to work with students who learn or behave differently. As a result, the school day can be very frustrating for both regular educators and students with ADHD.

Now picture that instead of spending just a few hours a day with these challenging students, you have to spend most of your life with them. This is exactly what parents and siblings of children with ADHD do. Moreover, if regular educators have very little training regarding children with special needs, family members tend to have much less.

One more visualization. Picture yourself as a special educator. You have just graduated from college with honors and been offered hundreds of jobs throughout the world. You are well versed in various disabling conditions, teaching strategies, behavior modification techniques, assessment procedures, and accommodations. In short, you are just an incredible source of information and inspiration. Additionally, being the great collaborator that you are, you work closely with classroom teachers to help develop educational programs that empower regular educators to teach and students with ADHD to learn. In fact, due solely to your tireless labors, you enable teachers and students to prosper in a world full of bliss. Is your job done? Not by a long shot.

What about the family? Chances are family members of students will need just as much assistance, if not more, as regular educators. For example, parents need to understand what ADHD is, what causes it, how it is treated, conditions that are commonly associated with ADHD, characteristics of people with ADHD, and—most importantly—how to teach and discipline their child. Do not forget that most learning occurs outside of classrooms and that parents are the first and primary teachers of all children.

By focusing on both school and home, you can increase the potential of children with ADHD. Students cannot learn effectively at school if they are having problems at home. Further, many of the behavioral modification programs that teachers create won't be effective if they are only used in classrooms. It is necessary for teachers and parents to work together to prepare students with ADHD for their futures.

In an effort to help you work with individuals with ADHD—in whatever role you may have—this text has three primary goals:

1. To inform you of key information regarding ADHD (e.g., its causes, characteristics, and treatments).
2. To give you strategies that can help students with ADHD maximize their abilities so that they can function better at school and at home, thus making ADHD a gift—not a disability.
3. To give you the skills needed to develop, implement, and evaluate educational programs that are based upon the needs of individuals with ADHD.

WHAT ARE "ATTENTION DEFICIT HYPERACTIVITY DISORDERS"?

The first question that you are probably asking yourself is "What are attention deficit hyperactivity disorders?" By this you mean either, "What are examples of different types of attention deficit hyperactivity disorders?" or "How are various attention disorders defined?" Let's start with the examples and then move to the actual definitions.

Attention deficit hyperactivity disorders are comprised of several disorders affecting an individual's ability to focus and maintain attention. Perhaps you have heard of attention deficit hyperactivity disorder (ADHD) or attention deficit disorder (ADD). These are two different, though related, classifications of attention disorders. Unfortunately, people use these terms interchangeably. Perhaps a brief history lesson will help.

A Brief History of Attention Deficit Hyperactivity Disorders

Prior to the 1980s, there was no ADD or ADHD. That is, these terms were not yet popularized. At that time, individuals with attention problems might have been diagnosed with "minimal brain dysfunction." The idea back then was that children who had problems paying attention or were hyperactive had slight brain injuries, possibly caused during birth. However, by the 1980s, minimal brain dysfunction gave way to the terms "attention deficit disorder" and "attention deficit hyperactivity disorder."

ADD described persons who were "spacey" or "inattentive." For example, a child who just sat in her chair at school and daydreamed or lost her toys at home might have met the criteria for ADD. Children who were constantly out of their seats, running around, or doing things without thinking of the consequences might have been considered ADHD. In other words, ADHD was used for people who where "overactive" or "impulsive."

But don't get to used to the term ADD. It isn't used anymore, at least not correctly. You see, in 1994 the American Psychiatric Association (APA) redefined attention deficit disorders so that there is no ADD. Instead, the APA broke ADHD into four "types" of attention disorders:

Types of Attention Deficit Hyperactivity Disorders

According to APA's most recent definition (2000), attention disorders can be subdivided into four types:

1. Attention Deficit Hyperactivity Disorder: Predominantly Inattentive Type (ADHD-I)
2. Attention Deficit Hyperactivity Disorder: Predominantly Hyperactive-Impulsive Type (ADHD-HI)
3. Attention Deficit Hyperactivity Disorder: Combined Type (ADHD-C)
4. Attention Deficit Hyperactivity Disorder: Not Otherwise Specified (ADHD-NOS)

Of the three main types of ADHD (i.e., ADHD-I, -HI, -C), most children have ADHD-C, as illustrated in figure 1.2 (McBurnett 1995). Further, males with ADHD outnumber females by as much as nine to one (American Psychiatric Association 2000; Barkley 1990). Out of the three main types of ADHD, females are more likely to have ADHD-I than ADHD-HI or ADHD-C, whereas males usually have ADHD-C.

Defining Attention Deficit Hyperactivity Disorders

Now let's go to the second question, "How are these disorders defined?" The American Psychiatric Association (APA) publishes a manual called *Diagnostic and Statistical Manual of Mental Disorders* or DSM. In it, you will find the criteria used to diagnose attention deficit

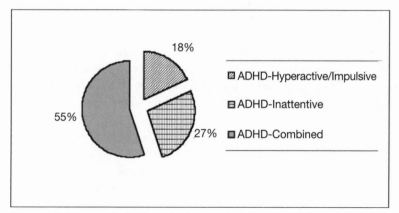

Figure 1.2   *Percent of Individuals with Attention Deficit Hyperactivity Disorder by Type*
Source: McBurnett (1995)

disorders, as well as many others. However, be aware that APA frequently updates the manual, so make sure you use the most current edition. Presently, the DSM is on its fourth edition.

DSM-IV defines ADHD-I as the following:

> Six or more of the following symptoms that have persisted for at least 6 months to a degree that is maladaptive and inconsistent with the individual's developmental level:

1. often fails to give close attention to details or makes careless mistakes in schoolwork, work, or other activities
2. often has difficulty sustaining attention for tasks or play activities
3. often does not seem to listen when spoken to directly
4. often does not follow through on instructions and fails to finish schoolwork, chores, or duties in the workplace
5. often has difficulty organizing tasks and activities
6. often avoids, dislikes, or is reluctant to engage in tasks that require sustained mental effort (such as schoolwork or homework)
7. often loses things necessary for tasks or activities (such as toys, pencils, or school assignments)
8. is often easily distracted by extraneous stimuli
9. is often forgetful of daily activities.

ADHD-HI is defined by DSM-IV as:

> Six or more of the following symptoms that have persisted for at least 6 months to a degree that is maladaptive and inconsistent with the individual's developmental level:

1. often fidgets with hands or feet or squirms in seat
2. often leaves seat in classroom or in other situations in which remaining seated is expected (e.g., church)
3. often runs about or climbs excessively in situations in which it is inappropriate (for adolescents and adults, this may be limited to subjective feelings of restlessness)
4. often has difficult playing or engaging in leisure activities quietly
5. is often "on the go" or often acts as if "driven by a motor"
6. often talks excessively
7. often blurts out answers before questions have been completed
8. often has difficulty awaiting turn
9. often interrupts or intrudes on others

If somebody meets the criteria for both ADHD-I and ADHD-HI, they could be diagnosed with ADHD-C (i.e., attention deficit hyperactivity disorder—combined). Further, if they come very close to fulfilling the diagnostic criteria for ADHD-I, ADHD-HI, or ADHD-C, but do not exhibit enough of the symptoms, they could be diagnosed with ADHD-NOS (i.e., attention deficit hyperactivity disorder-not otherwise specified). In other words, ADHD-NOS is a catch-all category for individuals who are obviously having difficult with their attention but do not officially meet the criteria for other attention deficit hyperactivity disorders (table 1.1).

Other Requirements for Diagnosis

Present before age seven.   In addition to having six or more of the symptoms outlined above, people with ADHD (e.g., ADHD-I, -HI, -C, or -NOS) must also meet several other requirements. First, some of the symptoms that cause the impairment must have been present before age seven. This is not to say that ADHD cannot be diagnosed later on in life. In fact, many individuals are diagnosed with ADHD well into their adulthood. However, the primary symptoms must be evident during childhood.

Table 1.1   Defining Characteristics of Each Type of Attention Deficit Disorder

ADHD-I	ADHD-HI	ADHD-C	ADHD-NOS
Inattentive	Hyperactive Impulsive	Inattentive Hyperactive Impulsive	Inattentive Hyperactive Impulsive

Note: Severity of characteristics present in ADHD-NOS are less severe, or less numerous, than those associated with ADHD-C.

Numerous settings.   Second, the symptoms of ADHD must be present in numerous settings. Consider how you behave during a boring conversation or movie. You probably fidget, miss details, have difficulty sustaining attention, as well many other symptoms of ADHD. However, this does not mean you have ADHD. Conversely, if a child who actually has ADHD is on the playground, his symptoms may not be as evident as they are in your classroom. In other words, the environment plays a substantial role in how ADHD manifests itself. Therefore, as we discuss throughout this text, you must consider environmental factors when developing strategies to help individuals with ADHD.

Clinical impairment.   Third, in order to be diagnosed with ADHD, there must be convincing evidence of clinically significant impairment to social, academic, or occupational functioning. In other words, if a child is just mildly distractible, she probably shouldn't be diagnosed with ADHD. More than likely, her distractibility is a facet of her personality or the result of other factors, such as lack of sleep. In order to be diagnosed with ADHD, her distractibility would have to negatively affect her life to such a degree that it impairs her ability to achieve her goals, such as doing well in school or at work.

Other disorders.   Fourth, symptoms associated with ADHD must not be caused by other conditions, such as schizophrenia, anxiety disorders, or mood disorders. This is important because many disorders mimic symptoms of ADHD. For example, individuals with schizophrenia might be inattentive because the "voices" in their heads are distracting them. Further, a person who is very anxious might fidget or appear hyperactive, just like somebody with ADHD. Unfortunately, misdiagnosis is very common.

It is, therefore, very important for teachers and parents to continuously reevaluate the diagnoses of their students. No diagnosis is set in stone. Further, many criteria for conditions, such as ADHD, change over time. As a result, an individual may be diagnosed with ADHD one year, but not the next. Even if a student has had the same diagnosis during childhood, it isn't uncommon for his or her diagnosis to change several times later in life.

To illustrate the importance of catching misdiagnoses, imagine for a moment how you would treat a child who is depressed and staring off into space. Now picture another child with ADHD-I who is also staring off into space. Your educational program—that is, the strategies, activities, and accommodations—that you develop for each of these children is probably very different. For example, you might refer the depressed student for counseling or group therapy while developing a behavior modification plan for the student with ADHD-I.

Now imagine that you accidentally switched the two conditions. The student who you thought had ADHD-I is actually staring off into space because she is depressed and the student who you thought was depressed actually has ADHD-I. Do the educational programs that you developed for them address the students' needs? Probably not. Depression is unlikely to change because of a behavior modification plan and, although counseling may help a student with ADHD-I, it is doubtful that it will completely rectify his condition.

Frequency of behavior.   Notice that the criteria for ADHD say "often fidgets" or "often talks excessively." They do not say "always fidgets" or "always talks excessively." This is very important point to remember. If somebody is diagnosed with ADHD, it does not mean that he or she can't sit still or be quiet. In fact, they might become so engrossed in a video game or a book that it is difficult to get their attention.

Think of it this way. Everybody has difficulty sitting still at times, especially during boring lectures or long movies. However, for people with ADHD-HI or ADHD-C, sitting still is more difficult than for most people. For instance, a person without ADHD might be able to sit for ten or fifteen minutes without moving; a person with ADHD-HI, however, might only be able to sit quietly for a minute or two.

With respect to impulsivity, everybody says things that they regret from time to time. Comments sometimes pop out of people's mouths before they are able to stop them, especially if they have consumed some alcohol or are tired. This is just natural. People with ADHD, though, say things without thinking more frequently than the rest of the population.

In other words, the key to defining ADHD is not the behavior per se, but the frequency of behavior. Moreover, the behavior must occur frequently enough to somehow impair the person's functioning. In a sense, we all display ADHD-like symptoms every now and then. What separates people with ADHD from everybody else is how often these behaviors occur and whether they affect their lives.

Developmental level.   The definition of ADHD also takes into consideration the developmental level of the individual. Suppose that you were at a party and that a friend of yours kept interrupting you every time you were telling a story or responding to a question. Perhaps he even touched you inappropriately or talked excessively about nothing in particular. Now picture that you were at a family reunion and that one of your cousins acted exactly like your friend. However, your cousin is only three years old and your friend in his twenties. Is there a difference in their behavior? Definitely!

Society has different expectations of children and adults. A three-year-old child is expected to interrupt and to do things that are inappropriate; adults should be able to control their actions. Therefore, in order to be diagnosed with ADHD, you have to exhibit behaviors that are atypical for people your age and situation. In order to have ADHD, a person's behavior will have to be different from other three- or twenty-year-olds.

In summary, there are many diverse types of attention deficit hyperactivity disorders. Further, the names and criteria of these disorders change frequently—thus causing considerable confusion in the media and the field of education. Throughout this text, we will focus on the four conditions that are collectively called ADHD: ADHD-I (predominately inattentive), ADHD-HI (predominately hyperactive-impulsive), ADHD-C (combined), and ADHD-NOS (not otherwise specified). Each of these conditions manifests itself in different ways. Your ability to develop appropriate educational programs may be the key to whether your student or child will succeed later in life.

WHAT CAUSES ATTENTION DEFICIT HYPERACTIVITY DISORDERS?

The next question you probably have is "What causes ADHD?" or "Why is my child like this?" Unfortunately, answering these questions is somewhat problematic for at least two reasons.

As you know, the definition of ADHD has changed frequently over the past ten years. As a result, it is difficult to conduct valid studies when the subject matter is as elusive as ADHD. Second, there is no single cause of ADHD. For instance, if there are four or five students with ADHD in a classroom, it is likely that their conditions have different, and multiple, causes. These causes can be broken into two broad categories: nongenetic factors and genetic factors.

Nongenetic Causes of ADHD

Many nongenetic factors are often associated with ADHD. These include parenting styles, socioeconomic status, and family structure. Several studies have found that parents of children without ADHD discipline their children differently than parents of children with ADHD (Barkley 1990; Barkley, Karlsson, and Pollard 1985; Cunningham and Barkley 1978). However, these studies concluded that such differences were the result of having children with attention deficit hyperactivity disorders, and not the cause of the disorders themselves. Still, the discipline techniques used by parents undoubtedly affect their children's behaviors.

In addition to parental styles, the development of ADHD is likely to be linked to prenatal and perinatal variables, such as anoxia (Barkley, DuPaul, and McMurray 1990; Sprich-Buckminster et al. 1993). Fetuses who do not get enough oxygen as they develop often will develop ADHD-like symptoms, including problems with impulse control and attention. Consequently, many people still believe that there is an association between brain injury and ADHD.

Further, ADHD has been thought to be caused by allergies or the child's diet. Research, however, has not been able to support these last two beliefs (Conners 1980; McGee, Stanton, and Sears 1993). In fact, in order for a child to become hyperactive throughout the day, for most days, they would have to ingest massive amounts of sugar or caffeine, so much so that they would likely become very ill. Moreover, if a child is hyperactive only after he eats a certain food (e.g., nuts), the symptoms probably would not be frequent enough to adversely affect his life. As a result, he shouldn't be misdiagnosed with ADHD.

Genetic Causes of ADHD

Genetics is also thought to be a significant predictor of ADHD. Several studies involving twins have found strong evidence of a genetic predisposition for ADHD (Gilger, Pennington, and DeFries 1992; Goodman and Stevenson 1989; Heffron, Martin, and Welsh 1984). In fact, studies have estimated that 20 to 30 percent of children with ADHD have family members with the disorder (Biederman et al.1986; Biederman et al. 1991; Frick et al. 1991).

The genetic etiology of ADHD, though, is still a mystery. However, thanks to new technological advances in medicine, growing evidence is supporting the notion that structural or morphological abnormalities in the brain may be the primary cause of ADHD. Studies using positron emission tomographic (PET) scans and magnetic resonance imaging (MRI) are beginning to identify differences in the brains of children with ADHD compared to the brains of children without ADHD symptoms (Mann et al. 1992). Simply put, the frontal lobes and brain stem regions are different in the brains of persons diagnosed with ADHD than the brains of control groups (Amen, Paldi, and Thisted 1993; Hynd et al. 1993; Hynd, Hern, Voeller, and Marshall 1991; Zametkin et al. 1990). Exactly how these variations in brain structure influence a person's behavior or lead to ADHD is still unknown.

Outgrowing ADHD

Another question you might have regarding ADHD is "Will my child out grow it?" Although it was once believed that symptoms of ADHD diminished with time, recent studies have found that ADHD does not go away (Fischer et al. 1993). However, after leaving the structured confines of classrooms, adults with ADHD often find themselves in environments better suited to their needs. For example, suppose that a child with ADHD has trouble sitting still or paying attention. However, when that same person graduates, she may get a job where she doesn't have to sit still (e.g., professional athlete, teacher, mechanic). Thus, the problems associated with ADHD (e.g., fidgeting, restlessness, and difficulty paying attention) are not as apparent as before—giving the appearance that she "outgrew" ADHD.

In summary, nobody really can say for sure what causes ADHD. Current theories suggest that ADHD is a lifelong, inherited condition caused predominately by abnormalities in the structure of the brain. This is not to say that individuals with ADHD are brain damaged, nor should parents feel a sense of blame for their child's condition. As we will discuss throughout this book, ADHD, if treated and approached correctly, can be viewed as a gift. In fact, few "normal" people can match the energy and creativity that individuals with ADHD possess. It is the job of teachers and parents to help children harness this energy and maximize their abilities.

HOW ARE ATTENTION DEFICIT
HYPERACTIVITY DISORDERS DIAGNOSED?

You might be asking yourself, "What do I do if I think one of my students or children has ADHD?" The first step is to collect information. A good place to begin is the criteria listed in DSM-IV. Do they describe the child? Even if they describe your student to a T, you can't stop there.

Behavioral Rating Scales

You also should use a variety of rating scales in order to measure the child's behaviors at school, home, and other environments. Numerous people, such as regular educators, teaching assistants, parents, and other family members should complete these scales. Available scales include:

- ADD-H: Comprehensive Teacher Rating Scale (ACTeRS) (Ullmann, Slator, and Sprague 1991)
- ADHD Rating Scale (DuPaul 1991)
- Attention Deficit Disorder Evaluation Scale-School Version (ADDES) (McCarney 1989)
- Attention-Deficit/Hyperactivity Disorder Test (Gilliam 1995)
- Behavior Assessment System for Children-Teacher Rating Scales (BASC-TRS) (Reynolds and Kamphaus 1992)
- Child Behavior Checklist-Teacher's Report Form (CBCL-TRF) (Achenbach 1991)
- Conners Teacher Rating Scales (CTRS) (Conners 1989)
- Devereux Behavior Rating Scale-School Form (DBRS-SF) (Naglieri, LeBuffe, and Pfeiffer 1994)

Interviewing Students, Families, and Peers

In addition to observing the student and completing behavioral rating scales, you should also interview the student, various family members, and the student's peers. Each may have important insights as to the child's actions. Interviews can be formal or informal. The result, however, should be an honest picture of what is going on as well as possible explanations and potential strategies.

Review Records

You will also need to review the student's records and perform a battery of standard tests, such as medical, intelligence, and aptitude exams. From these, you should be able to rule out other explanations for the student's behavior. For example, it may be that a student is inattentive because of hearing loss and not because of ADHD. Further, by examining the student's past work, you can determine whether the student's behaviors are recent or ongoing.

Clinical Assessments

Finally, there are several clinical assessments for which you can refer students. One group of assessments is called "continuous performance tests" (CPT). With these, the student would sit in front of a computer and watch letters flash on the screen. When a specific letter appears, the student is to push a designated key, such as the space bar. This procedure measures the student's ability to focus attention by recording how many times the student "forgot" to push the key as well as how many times he pushed the key erroneously.

Other clinical assessments could include neuropsychological examinations. A neuropsychologist should perform medical tests to rule out any medical condition that might be causing the concern. For example, the doctor might conduct an EEG, MRI, or a CAT scan to see if the student has a traumatic brain injury.

Interpreting the Data

After all of this diverse information is collected, the most important part of the assessment process begins—interpreting the data. This means that you, family members, the student, the doctors, school psychologist, and other personnel have to make sense of what has been learned. In some cases, it might be clear to everybody that the student has ADHD. In most cases, however, the proper diagnosis—if any—is less obvious. Further, as with all conditions, you must consider cultural issues that might explain a student's behavior. Only when you have a clear understanding of the students' behaviors will you be able to develop an effective treatment (i.e., education program).

CULTURAL DIVERSITY AND ADHD

Different people learn in different ways. Some people are auditory learners; others need to see something in order to understand it. This is pretty common sense. However, in addition to individual differences, there frequently are differences based on cultural backgrounds.

For example, suppose that you had a student who never looked at you while you were talking. What would you think? Would you ask the student to pay attention? What about a student who never said anything in class, but just sat there looking at you with wide, blinking eyes? Would you think this student was stoned? How about a student who frequently talked in class while he was supposed to be doing seat work and was often fidgeting? Does this student have ADHD-HI?

Each of the behaviors described about could be the result of disability, substance abuse, or cultural upbringing. For instance, the student who isn't looking at you might have ADHD-I and, as a result, might not be paying attention. Another explanation is that the student is African American and she might be displaying culturally learned behavior. That is, African Americans are more likely to look away from a speaker to whom they are listening than Anglo-Americans (Sue and Sue 1990).

How about a student who just stares at you, blinking? It could be that she is on drugs or has ADHD-I. It could also be that the student is Native American. In many Native American cultures, authority figures (such as teachers and adults in general) are revered. Further, the appropriate response to an authority figure is to maintain eye contact and to blink. In essence, blinking is used much like many Anglo cultures use nodding their head to encourage speakers to go on (Sue and Sue 1990).

How about the student who is talkative and prone to fidgeting? Although excessive talking and movement is a key characteristic of ADHD-HI, it could be that his behavior is related to his culture. For example, Hispanic students, especially those from Puerto Rican families, display more body language and talk more than students of typical Anglo backgrounds (Bauermeister 1995). In one study, White teachers misdiagnosed one-quarter of Puerto Rican students with ADHD (Williams, Lerner, Wigal, and Swanson 1995).

The bottom line is this. Before you diagnose a student as having ADHD, gain an understanding of that student's cultural background. Try to rule out any cultural influences that might influence his behavior. But also remember that culture is not defined by the color of somebody's skin. Culture is influenced by socioeconomic status, region of the country, gender, as well as many other factors. Misdiagnosis of ADHD is very common. Careful consideration of cultural issues can help your students obtain the service that they need to succeed in life.

HOW ARE ATTENTION DEFICIT
HYPERACTIVITY DISORDERS TREATED?

Treatment of ADHD is far more important than its etiology, especially to parents and teachers who are primarily concerned with the child's long-term future. Effective treatment has been found to contain four components: medication, behavioral-cognitive modifications, accommodations, and parental training (Anastopoulos et al. 1993). When treating individuals with ADHD, a multidimensional treatment is the best; try to use all four of these approaches in unison.

Throughout the remainder of this book, we will be discussing strategies and accommodations that can be used with students with ADHD of various ages, both in their classrooms and at their homes. You will also learn how to evaluate these strategies to see if they are accomplishing their goals.

Medication

The most popular forms of medication for ADHD are stimulants, such as methylphenidate (Ritalin), dexroampetamine (Dexedrine), and pemoline (Cylert). You may be surprised that stimulants are used to treat people with ADHD since stimulants, such as amphetamines or "speed," make most people more energetic. More energy is the last thing that a child with ADHD needs. For people with ADHD, however, stimulants have been found to increase attention and decrease both activity and impulsivity (Anastopoulos et al. 1993). They have also been found to improve the compliance of children with ADHD (Barkley 1989) as well as to reduce aggressive behavior (Hinshaw et al. 1989).

As with most medications, stimulants have many side effects. For example, 30 percent of students experience a "rebound effect," which means that as the drug wears off, the student's behavior becomes worse than it would have been without the medication (DuPaul, Barkley, and McMurray 1991). Children could also experience depression, headaches, reduced appetite, weight loss, stomach cramps, and irritability (Fine and Johnston 1993). Additionally, after long-term use, even normal doses of stimulants can slow physical growth (Roche et al. 1979). It is for these reasons that most children with ADHD do not take their medications during the summer. This respite gives their bodies a break from the chemicals and helps prevent tolerance, which would result in the need to increase dosage levels.

Approximately one third of children with ADHD do not respond well to stimulants (Biederman et al. 1989). Of these, most are treated with antidepressants, such as Tofanil (imipramine) and Norpramin (desipramine). These medications are also used for individuals who have both ADHD and depression or anxiety disorders. Unfortunately, the use of antidepressants raises concerns given the numerous, and potentially severe, side effects that these medications might present. Such side effects may include an increase in blood pressure as well as damage to the kidneys and heart (DuPaul and Stoner 1994). Table 1.2 provides an overview of the common medications used to treat ADHD and their potential positive and negative effects.

In addition to the problems associated with side effects, overmedication, and inappropriate medication, the use of drugs has several shortcomings. For instance, although medications may decrease activity and increase attention, they will not teach children social skills or how to follow directions. Further, medication will not help students obtain knowledge missed prior to medical treatment.

At this point, you might be wondering, "What do I need to do regarding my student's medications?" For instance, are you supposed to give them out? What do you do if your student is having a bad reaction to his or her medications? What if your student's medications aren't working? These are only some of the issues that arise when pharmaceuticals are utilized.

Typically, nurses or school administrators keep and distribute medications if students need to take them during school hours. For the most part, the role of teachers and parents is to monitor the effects of the medications on their students' behavior and learning. This is important for two reasons. First, as discussed earlier, medications have many side effects; several could be very serious. You must help identify side effects before they become dangerous. Therefore, you will need to become acquainted with the medications that your student is taking as well as know what to look for should side effects begin to emerge.

Second, whether you are a parent or teacher, you will need to help physicians determine if medications are working. To do this, you will have to assess the behavior of your student before and after medications are prescribed. The behavior of the student on medication is then compared to behavior prior to medication. You also must compare the ideal behavior to the actual behavior. In this manner, you can determine whether medications are having their desired effect at their current dosage levels.

Table 1.2   Medication Used to Treat ADHD and Their Potential Side Effects

Brand name (generic) type of medication form	Positives	Negatives	Notes
Catapress (Clonidine) Antihypertensive patches & tablets	Patches last five to six days. Few serious side effects.	Patches are costly. Tablets last only four hours.	Effective with defiant behavior. Can be used with Tourette's syndrome.
Cylert (Pemoline) Psychostimulant tablets	Lasts up to eight hours. Reduces hyperactivity.	Takes three to four hours to begin working. Can cause liver damage, seizures, and hallucinations.	Requires blood work every six months.
Dexedrine (Dextroamphetamine) Psychostimulant tablets	Fast acting (within an hour). Reduces hyperactivity.	Lasts for hours. High doses can cause depression and fatigue.	Not recommended for children under six years old.
Lithium (Eskalith) Antidepressant tablets	Diminishes manic episodes. Reduces depression.	Not for children under twelve years old. May cause thirst and diarrhea.	Requires blood work every six months. Side effects decrease over time.
Norpramin and Tofranil (Imipramine and Despipramine) Antidepressants tablets	Last up to twenty-four hours. Likely to improve depression and mood disorders.	May take four weeks to reach full effect. May cause anxiety and insomnia.	Must be monitored closely by doctors. Used when stimulants are ineffective. Students must be weaned on and off medications.
Ritalin (Methylphenidate) Psychostimulant tablets	Works within thirty minutes. Sustained release tablets last up to eight hours.	Regular tablets last four hours. May cause tics, insomnia, and nervousness.	Very commonly used.
Wellbutrin (Bupropion) Aminoketones tablets	May reduce hyperactivity, anxiety and aggression.	Can cause insomnia, headaches, gastrointestinal distress, seizures.	Mostly used with adults.

Sources:
Bender, W. N. *Understanding ADHD: A Practical Guide for Teachers and Parents.* (Upper Saddle River, N.J.: Merrill/Prentice Hall, 1997).
Dowdy, C. A., J. R. Patton, T. E. C. Smith, and E. A. Polloway. *Attention-Deficit/Hyperactivity Disorder in the Classroom.* (Austin, Tex.: PRO-ED, 1998).
Lerner, J. W., B. Lowenthal, and S. R. Lerner. *Attention Deficit Disorders: Assessment and Teaching.* (Pacific Grove, Calif.: Brooks/Cole, 1995).

Behavioral-Cognitive Modification

Medication is most effective when it is used in conjunction with behavioral-cognitive modifications (Barkley 1995). Behavioral-cognitive modifications tend to focus on teaching students self-control or self-monitoring. They can also include strategies for teaching students alternatives to inappropriate behaviors. For example, teachers and parents could use a token economy system where children with ADHD are rewarded for completing homework assignments or acting appropriately with peers.

Accommodations

Accommodations help students circumvent problem areas that are not corrected by medication or behavioral-cognitive strategies. For instance, suppose that a student is failing math. It is not that she can't do the work, she can. But after completing a few problems correctly, she gets distracted and makes careless mistakes on all the rest of the problems. An accommodation for this student might be to have her do only a few problems at a time. Perhaps she could complete three or four problems, work on English for a few minutes, and then come back to math a little later.

Parental Training

Finally, the most important teachers that children will ever have are their parents. Unfortunately, parents frequently do not understand ADHD nor do they possess the knowledge needed to adequately teach or discipline their children. To help make ADHD a gift, you may need to educate family members about their child's condition and to share with them strategies that can improve the child's behavior. The following chapters will help you in this endeavor.

WHAT OTHER CONDITIONS ARE ASSOCIATED WITH ADHD?

In order to develop and implement effective educational programs for students with ADHD, you will need to understand not only ADHD but also the conditions that frequently coincide with it. For example, studies have found that 25 to 65 percent of children with ADHD also have oppositional-defiant disorder (ODD) and most have significant problems with aggression (Barkley, DuPaul, and McMurray 1990; DuPaul and Stoner 1994; McGee et al. 1991). With this in mind, how would you discipline a student with ADHD who is apparently ignoring your directions (e.g., "Take your seat," "Turn in your homework," "Complete the following problems")?

Before you decide how you are going to act, you might first want to ask yourself some questions. For example, is he not following directions because he was distracted and didn't hear you (which might be caused by the ADHD)? Or is he not following your directions in an effort to irritate you or get you off task (which might be caused by the ODD)? Think about those questions for a moment. What you perceive as the root cause of a student's behavior will guide your actions. If your perceptions are wrong, you are unlikely to correct the behavior problems and teach your student effectively.

In addition to ODD, studies have found that between 30 and 50 percent of children with ADHD also have learning disabilities (Barkley, DuPaul, and McMurray 1990; DuPaul and Stoner 1994; Fletcher, Shaywitz, and Shaywitz 1994; McGee et al. 1991). As with ODD, the presence of learning disabilities could exacerbate your efforts to assess the abilities and needs of students, as well as to formulate educational programs (figure 1.3). Determining whether a student's behaviors are caused by ADHD or by a learning disability, however, is difficult given

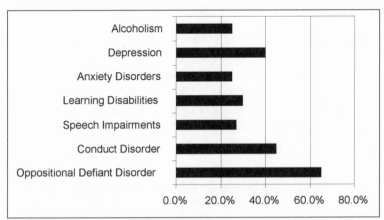

Figure 1.3 *Percent of Individuals with ADHD Who Have Additional Conditions*
Sources:
Bender, W. N. Understanding ADHD: A Practical Guide for Teachers and Parents. (Upper Saddle River, NJ.: Merrill/Prentice Hall, 1997).
Dowdy, C. A., J. R. Patton, T. E. C. Smith, and E. A. Polloway. Attention-Deficit/Hyperactivity Disorder in the Classroom. (Austin, Tex.: PRO-ED, 1998).

the similarities between the two conditions. In the end, it is a good idea to examine the strengths of all students and to present information using the strategies that best match the student's learning style.

Remember the example we discussed earlier about the two students, one with depression and the other with ADHD-I? Unfortunately, depression is another condition that people with ADHD often experience, especially adolescents and adults with ADHD-I (Barkley 1995). Depression is a very serious issue. If you ever notice that a child appears to be devoid of positive feelings for days on end or whether his or her affect has changed, seek help immediately. Talk with the school nurse, counselor, or psychologist. It is far better to overreact to depression than to not act at all.

Individuals with ADHD are also at risk for sleep disorders, bed wetting during childhood, and substance abuse (Conners and Wells 1986).

IDENTIFYING DEPRESSED STUDENTS

One of the most common conditions that students with ADHD are likely to have is depression. According to the DSM-IV, depression is a recurring condition lasting at least two weeks where a minimum of four of the following conditions are consistently present:

1. loss of interest or pleasure in all or most activities
2. change in appetite or weight
3. loss of energy
4. thoughts of death or suicide
5. listlessness or agitation
6. insomnia or hypersomnia
7. feelings of worthlessness or excessive guilt
8. diminished ability to think or concentrate
9. feelings of sadness or of being "empty"

If one of your students comes close to meeting this criterion, it is very important that you seek help as soon as possible. This is especially true for students who have been depressed for several weeks but suddenly appear fine. Abrupt improvements in mood or disposing of once important possessions often signal that the student has decided to commit suicide. If you ever have any doubts about the emotional state of your students, contact the school psychologist or counselor immediately. It is better to be safe than to be sorry.

In fact, people with ADHD are commonly found to have additive personalities. That is, they are more likely to gamble excessively, shop compulsively, or work too hard (Wender 1987). Addressing these issues with the student as early as possible is very important so that steps can be taken to prevent future abuse. (For more information regarding sleep disorders see the boxed discussion here; for more information regarding substance abuse, see the boxed discussion in chapter 7.)

Having ADHD is not all bad, however. There have been many successful people who have had ADHD, such as actor/comedian Robin

---

HELPING STUDENTS WITH SLEEP DIFFICULTIES

In addition to depression, students with ADHD are likely to have difficulty sleeping. This is particularly true for hyperactive students who are unable to relax. For instance, when they lie in their beds, hyperactive students still have the urge to tap their fingers or bounce their knees. Further, hyperactive students are unable to "turn off" their minds at the end of the day. Consequently, many students might take several hours to fall asleep, making concentrating the next morning difficult: Here are several tips to help students who have sleeping problems:

- Exercise regularly, but not within six hours of going to bed.
- Try new bedding, such as a firmer mattress or softer blanket.
- Noise and light should be kept to a minimum. However, "white noise" such as soft background music can often help people fall asleep.
- Hide the clock. Put it underneath the bed or in a drawer so it doesn't become a reminder to the student that he isn't falling asleep.
- Keep a regular sleep schedule. Get up at the same time every day, even on weekends.
- Don't take naps during the day.
- Perform presleep rituals, such as relaxation exercises, to help transition the body into a sleeping mode.
- Do not eat or drink within three hours of going to bed.
- Go to bed only when tired.
- Do not lie awake in bed for more than twenty minutes. Get up, watch television or read, and return to bed when tired.
- Do not do anything in bed other than sleep. Do not watch television, study, or eat.
- Do not take sleeping pills in conjunction with medication for ADHD unless approved by a doctor.

Sources:

Bowles, W. V., and C. G. Wirth, *Insomnia Plus ... : The Answer to Sleeplessness.* (Tulsa, Okla.: Temple Treasures, 1990).

DiGeronimo, T. F. *Insomnia: Fifty Essential Things to Do.* (New York: Plume, 1997).

Dunkell, S. *Goodbye Insomnia, Hello Sleep.* (New York: Carol Publishing, 1994).

Hauri, P., and S. Linde. *No More Sleepless Nights.* (New York: John Wiley, 1996).

Morin, C. M. *Relief from Insomnia: Getting the Sleep of Your Dreams.* (New York: Doubleday, 1996).

Williams. With the proper supports and necessary skills, ADHD could be considered a "super-ability"! In fact, several studies have found similarities between ADHD and giftedness (Leal, Kearney, and Kearney 1995; Webb and Latimer 1993). Remember, just because somebody is in special education doesn't mean that she is stupid. Students with ADHD, as well as those with learning disabilities and behavior disorders, frequently have IQs well into the gifted range. These students not only need strategies to help them learn, they also need to be challenged academically.

In summary, diagnosing and treating ADHD is often made difficult due to the many conditions with which it can coexist. For instance, individuals with ADHD-I are likely to suffer from clinical depression. Individuals with ADHD-HI, on the other hand, frequently have oppositional defiant disorder or conduct disorders. However, regardless of all the challenges students with ADHD may face, it is important to note that they have many strengths as well, such as being highly creative and intelligent. To help students succeed in life, you will have to assess the individual's needs and strengths, determine whether behavior is the result of mitigating circumstances (e.g., a secondary disability), and then develop educational programs that are most appropriate for the given situation.

WHAT ARE THE PRIMARY CHARACTERISTICS OF ADHD?

Students with ADHD tend to be somewhat complex. While creative and intelligent, they also can be academically erratic, immature, and prone to mood swings. Further, they are likely to have multiple disabilities ranging from depression to oppositional defiant disorders. However, many of the primary characteristics that individuals with ADHD display can be placed in four categories.

- Inattentive
- Impulsive
- Overactive
- Socially Inappropriate

Inattention

Inattention can manifest itself in several ways. For example, students may stare off into space. They could lose or misplace things. They can get math problems wrong because they missed important details. They could be very disorganized and have messy desks or homework. They could also have difficulty following directions.

Impulsive

Impulsivity can create some difficulties as well. For instance, students might blurt out answers or do things without thinking. Doing things without thinking is potentially dangerous. Imagine that students are conducting science experiments in their class and one of them suddenly wonders what a chemical tastes like or whether the Bunsen burner is hot. Before his brain can tell him not to do it, a student with ADHD is likely to have already burnt his hand or ingested poisonous material.

Overactive

Overactivity can include running, climbing, throwing projectiles, fidgeting, excessive talking, taking things apart, not being able to remain seated, constantly looking around, and thinking of many different things at the same time. Not only can these behaviors be annoying to the teacher and to other students, they could diminish the learning of the student with ADHD. Further, many of these behaviors may have biological causes that may limit how you address them. For instance, suppose a teacher has a student whose fidgeting is distracting the entire class. The teacher could warn the student that if she does not stop, she will be in time out. But it is very unlikely that the student would be able to stop fidgeting even if she tried. Further, sending her to time out only deprives her of an opportunity to learn. Additionally, the time out will not correct the problem of fidgeting.

Socially Inappropriate

Students with ADHD have often been described as rude, ill tempered, and socially immature. However, students with ADHD do not necessarily desire to be outcasts. Frequently, they fail to possess the skills needed to interact appropriately with peers. Further, their tendency to act impulsively, become distracted, and miss details may add to their inability to make and maintain friendships

All of these characteristics interrelate. For example, one of the reasons why students might have social deficits is because they are so impulsive. Further, the reason they might have difficulty maintaining their attention is that they are hyperactive. For this reason, the importance of a multidimensional approach when teaching students with ADHD cannot be understated.

Throughout this text, we will discuss ways of addressing problems associated with inattention, impulsivity, overactivity, and social deficits. Specifically, we will be developing methods of enhancing the environment, your teaching, and the student's skills. These methods can be utilized during various age levels in both the classroom and the home.

APPLYING WHAT YOU HAVE LEARNED

Look again at the case study of Mark at the beginning of the chapter. Do you think he has an attention deficit hyperactivity disorder? What evidence in the case study supports your assessment? How would you determine for sure whether Mark does, or does not, have ADHD? Are there any other possible explanations why Mark is behaving the way he is? If Mark does have ADHD, what type would you think he has? Finally, as a special education teacher, how would you help Mark's teacher?

Does Mark Have an Attention Deficit Disorder?

What is your conclusion? Does Mark have an attention deficit hyperactivity disorder? Let's take a look at the case study.

Although Mark certainly exhibits classical symptoms of ADHD (e.g., impulsivity, inattention, and hyperactivity), it is unclear if he should be diagnosed with an attention deficit hyperactivity disorder. First of all, the information provided pertains only to his behavior in the classroom. In order to be diagnosed with ADHD, symptoms must be present in several settings.

Secondly, we only have Mark's teacher's side of the story. Maybe he really isn't behaving any differently than his peers; perhaps the teacher just thinks that Mark is out of control.

Third, the case study made a passing reference to how Mark's grades were "beginning to slip." Although this comment alone does not preclude the possibility of ADHD, it should raise some doubts. Specifically, if Mark has ADHD, it is very likely that he would have had symptoms before turning twelve.

Further, by definition, in order to be diagnosed with ADHD, Mark's symptoms must be severe enough so that they impair his functioning. From the available information, we cannot be certain that Mark's difficulties aren't relatively recent or mild in nature. As a result, a diagnosis of any ADHD is premature.

How Would You Diagnose Mark?

How would you determine if Mark has ADHD or whether he was just a normal student or a student with another type of disability (e.g., schizophrenia)? There are several things that you should do. First, you should observe Mark in multiple environments, such as in class, at home, in the community, and during lunch.

Second, you should get more people involved in the process. You will need perceptions other than your own and those of Mark's teacher. Talk to Mark, his family members, siblings, and friends. What do they say? Does anybody else notice a problem? Have each person complete a behavioral rating form. Compare notes. Is there a pattern?

Third, review Mark's file. Did Mark's previous teachers document similar complaints? Did his grades slip during a certain point of the year, such as before spring break?

Finally, you may wish to refer Mark for a physical or neurological examination. See if Mark has any hearing loss or recent injury to the brain. These could help rule out an attention deficit hyperactivity disorder.

What Are Other Possible Explanations for Mark's Behavior?

Other than ADHD, what else can explain Mark's behaviors? The possibilities are limitless. However, you must be aware of other explanations for your student's actions. Not every child who is inattentive or hyperactive has ADHD. As a result, you must explore all plausible options.

Of course, this is purely speculation, but one plausible explanation for Mark's behaviors is that he is frustrated with school. Perhaps he is misbehaving to avoid work. The more frequently that he can get his teacher off task, the less material is actually covered.

Maybe Mark is becoming interested in girls and he doesn't know how to approach them. Think about it. Maybe the reason Mark is getting out of his seat is so that he can walk by the girl that he likes. Perhaps he isn't paying attention in class because he is daydreaming about her. Further, maybe he is bothering other female students in an effort to learn if she likes him. Remember, he is twelve years old. You probably exhibited the same (or similar) behaviors when you were his age. Not every behavior has to be the result of brain structure or antisocial tendencies.

What Type of ADHD Would Mark Have?

Let's suppose the Mark does have ADHD. What type of ADHD do you think he would likely have? ADHD-I? ADHD-HI? ADHD-C? Or ADHD-NOS?

Again, it is difficult to say for sure what Mark may or may not have, so let's go through Mark's symptoms. According to his teacher, Mark is inattentive in class and frequently forgets things. What type of ADHD do these symptoms indicate? One answer is ADHD-I or ADHD Predominantly Inattentive.

However, Mark's teacher also complains that he regularly gets out of his seat, blurts out comments, and talks excessively. What type of ADHD do these symptoms suggest? He could have ADHD-HI or ADHD Predominantly Hyperactive-Impulsive.

If Mark has both ADHD-I and ADHD-HI, does he then have two diagnoses? No. He would probably be diagnosed with ADHD-C or ADHD-Combined, which is a combination of inattentive and hyperactive-impulsive symptoms.

However, what if Mark's symptoms were relatively minor or did not completely fit the other categories? In these cases, Mark could be diagnosed with ADHD-NOS. "NOS" stands for "not otherwise specified" and it is used to indicate situations where an individual comes close but does not have all of the symptoms needed to be diagnosed with ADHD-I, ADHD-HI, or ADHD-C.

How Would You Help Mark's Teacher?

Whether as a teacher or a parent, you have an influential role in helping students with ADHD. Specifically, you have to help figure out how to adapt the classroom, modify teaching strategies, and determine what skills should be taught. What would you suggest that Mark's teacher do?

You might have Mark's teacher move Mark away from the girls he is constantly bothering, perhaps have Mark sit in the front of the room where the teacher has greater access to him. Further, if Mark can't sit still for more than fifteen minutes, have him run errands or hand out papers. To help him remember what he needs to bring to class, have him write down lists of "required materials" and "assignments that are due."

These are just a few suggestions that you could make to Mark's teacher. There are numerous others. Throughout the remainder of this text, you will learn of more strategies for particular problems (e.g., social skills) as well as strategies that can be used at various age levels (e.g., childhood). You will also learn how to evaluate strategies to determine whether they are working effectively.

CHAPTER 2

Methods of Addressing Inattention

CHAPTER OBJECTIVES

This chapter answers the following questions:

1. How can inattention be a problem?
2. How can the environment affect inattention?
3. How can teaching strategies affect inattention?
4. What skills are needed to improve inattention?

CASE STUDY: STACEY

I have a student whom really concerns me. Her name is Stacey. She is an ultra-shy fourteen-year-old female who is doing miserably in my English class. Actually, from what I understand, she is doing poorly in all of her subjects, especially math. Currently, the only courses that she is passing are science and physical education.

In her soft voice, Stacey has timidly told me that she likes English despite her present grade and spotty attendance. In fact, she says that it is her favorite subject, which surprises me since she doesn't appear to care for reading or writing, which is the lion's share of what we do in class. Further, when I am lecturing, she just stares out the window or at the chalkboard. When asked a direct question, she will reluctantly attempt to answer it; however, after a few moments, her responses become disjointed and turn into rambling sentences that are pointless and off topic. Additionally, she frequently needs reminding when assignments are due and she constantly leaves her work and books at home.

I suppose my biggest concern is how her classmates treat her. They tease her mercilessly and call her "stupid" and "Spacey Stacey." In fact, the only interactions that I have ever seen her have with her peers are negative and, as far as I know, she has no real friends. It is quite sad.

On the plus side, records indicate that Stacey has average intelligence and aptitude. Moreover, she comes from a fairly affluent family who seems to take an interest in her education. They are as concerned as I am since she behaves "strangely" at home as well. We are not sure what is wrong with her. All I know is that if something doesn't change, she will fail my class and be held back a year.

Case Study Questions

1. Do you think that Stacey has an attention deficit hyperactivity disorder? Explain.
2. Other than ADHD, what could be causing Stacey's behavior?
3. How could you modify Stacey's environments to help her become more attentive?
4. What strategies would you suggest her teachers utilize to help her pay attention?
5. What skills would you teach Stacey to help her improve her attention?

HOW CAN INATTENTION BE A PROBLEM?

As we have discussed earlier, inattention is a primary characteristic of individuals with ADHD. Outcomes of inattention include not participating in class, misplacing things (e.g., homework assignments or toys), missing details, or failing to follow directions. All of these outcomes are problematic, and if not addressed, could significantly affect the future of children with ADHD.

For example, suppose that every time you began to study for a big exam, you lost your class notes and textbooks. Would you do well in school? Imagine that whenever you try to find a friend's house, you only remember half of the directions or you don't pay attention to what street you are driving down. Would your social life suffer? Imagine during job interviews you mix up everybody's name and forget your résumé. Do you think you would get the job you wanted?

Inattention can be a significant problem for individuals with ADHD. From early childhood to late adulthood, inattention can adversely affect quality of life. For this reason, it is very important for people with ADHD to learn strategies that will minimize the damage caused by inattention. Further, these strategies must be taught as early in the person's life as possible, both at school and at home.

When addressing inattention, you will need to focus on three factors. The first is the environment, such as the student's classroom or bedroom. The second is your teaching. Whether you are an educator or parent, you'll need to examine the strategies, activities, and modalities of learning that you utilize. The third is the student. You'll need to teach the student efficient ways of organizing and processing information. These factors are interrelated. Therefore, in order to improve the students' attention, you must address their environments, your teaching, and their skills simultaneously.

HOW CAN THE ENVIRONMENT AFFECT INATTENTION?

Inattention can be a function of both distractibility and hyperactivity. A student who is running around the classroom is unlikely to attend to everything you say. Likewise, a student who is sitting by an open window facing a busy street is more apt to be focusing on the cars outside than on what you are teaching. Modifying the environment might help students pay attention to the lesson at hand.

Before we begin talking about how to modify classrooms, bedrooms, and other environments, be aware that—like all people—individuals with ADHD have different needs and different learning styles. What may work for one student may not work for another. However, through careful observation and assessment of the student's behaviors, you should be able to get an idea of where to begin.

Amount of Stimulation

Educators who work with children with ADHD have been asking themselves the age-old question "Should I have a lot of stimulation in my classroom or very little?" This is a very important question. Unfortunately, there is no absolute answer.

For just a second, put down this book and look around you. Describe it to yourself. Is the room big and airy or dark and cozy? Are you sitting in a comfortable chair? On the floor? Lying in bed? Do you have a lot of pictures on the walls? Are you facing a window? A corner? Is the light that you are using to read by filling the entire room or do you have a desk lamp that is illuminating only this page? Is the room cold?

Warm? Do you have snacks around you? Is the television on? Radio? Is it completely quiet?

If you are like many people, you prefer to have your environment a certain way when you are studying. For instance, some people have to hear noise, such as music or the television. Others have to go to the library where it is very quiet. The same is true for individuals with ADHD.

Some students with ADHD might be distracted in a classroom that has a lot of stimulation, such as posters, mobiles, and classroom pets. Others would go crazy without stimulation around them. So how do you figure out what is best for your students? Ask them. Experiment. Give them a desk in the corner where there is little stimulation and see how they do. Have them try to study at home with the radio on and see if it helps them focus.

What do you do if you have one student who can't take the stimulation and another who can't live without it? Do you have to have two separate classrooms? No. You can create study areas in the back of the room that suit the needs of your students. The idea is to create a place where your students can learn. Teaching students without such an environment is like pushing a shopping cart when all the wheels are going in different directions.

Seating Chart

Some students will need to be in the front of the classroom where other students do not distract them. Others need to be in the back of the classroom so that all of the stimulation is in front of them, thus reducing the desire to turn around to see what is going on behind them. A good compromise may be to arrange the room so that it is possible for a student to be at the front (where the teacher can redirect him, if needed) while also having no stimulation behind him. For example, arrange the desks in a horseshoe so that all students are facing the front of the room. Place the student with ADHD at the tip of the horseshoe closest to the teacher's desk. The proximity to the teacher might help him focus. Plus, with the wall to his back, there will be nothing behind him compelling him to turn around—thus taking his attention off of the assignment.

Using Study Carrels

Consider the other stimulation that might distract students with ADHD. Are there pictures on the walls? Mobiles hanging from the ceiling? Animals in cages? The hum of a fish tank or buzz of florescent lights? Should you have all of these things? Again, the answer is "it depends."

Think about the room in which you like to study. Is it completely devoid of stimulation? Could you study in a completely barren room? Just white walls, no furniture or pictures? Some of you are thinking, "Yeah, it *is* easier for me to concentrate that way." Others of you are repulsed at the thought of being confined to a room without color, pictures, or stimulation of any kind. The preferences of students with ADHD are likely to vary as well.

If a student does not like stimulation and finds it distracting, try putting her in a carrel or having her desk face a quiet corner. However, be careful not to single out the student or use her placement within the classroom as a way of making her different from her peers. Perhaps, several non-ADHD students would benefit from using a carrel or sitting facing the wall as well.

Suppose that a student can't do without stimulation. If you put her in an empty room, she would go crazy. Further, she actively seeks out stimulation when little is present. For instance, if she is sitting at her desk and there is nothing on the walls to occasionally glance at, she will stare out the window or draw pictures or do whatever it takes to give her mind the stimulation that it needs. If this is the case, you can still use a carrel. Simply allow her to decorate the inside of the carrel with pictures (perhaps even using pictures that relate to what you are teaching).

Quiet Areas

Another environmental modification that can help students concentrate is to have a designated quiet area. Perhaps you could use wall dividers and beanbag chairs where the students can sit and read. This strategy is useful at the student's home as well. There should be at least one room in the home that doesn't contain a television or radio. Further, this quiet area should be away from busy areas, such as the family room and kitchen.

Using Noise and Light

Perhaps all students could benefit from soft background noise or "white noise." For example, during quiet study time, you might want to play a CD of soft music or the sounds of waves, or allow students to listen to soft music via a Walkman when new information is not being presented. This could be very relaxing and help prevent external noise from distracting them. After a while, the music might "condition" students so that when the music begins playing they are calm and ready to work quietly at their desks.

Further, the use of lighting might help focus students' attention. For example, placing colored tissue paper over the outside covers of ceiling lights can make fluorescent lights less "harsh." The different colors might also create a friendlier, more relaxed atmosphere.

These concepts can easily be applied to the student's home. For example, maybe the reason the student doesn't do homework is because he finds it difficult to concentrate at home. Think about all the distracters at your home. There's the television, the refrigerator, the telephone, toys, the family pet, other family members who aren't studying, and there is often little structure—that is, nobody is going to refocus his attention if he begins staring off into space. Plus, the room of a child with ADHD is likely to resemble a disaster area. The desk is probably covered with dirty clothes, "lost" homework from several months back, toys, and things that you can't even imagine. It would be impossible for most people to study in that kind of environment, especially if they were highly distractible.

So let's change the home environment a little. Trying to get kids to clean their rooms is hard enough, so one way around it is to have the student do homework someplace else. For example, maybe the student could have a desk in the basement away from all of the distraction in his room. Perhaps, he could go to the local library. Further, a desk lamp might help him concentrate. The idea is to examine the learning needs of each student and try to find or create an environment that is suitable for learning.

HOW CAN TEACHING STRATEGIES AFFECT INATTENTION?

Now that you have examined and modified the student's environments so that potential distracters are minimized, you'll need to utilize strategies that can enhance your teaching. Many of these strategies will benefit students with and without disabilities. Further, many of them may seem to be common sense. However, when utilized as a package of diverse strategies, you are likely to increase the students' attention and learning.

Decreasing the Length of Instruction

If a student is having difficulty paying attention, you could decrease the length of time students are supposed to be working on a task. However, this does not mean that you should expect students with ADHD to do less work. Simply break up the time that they require to complete a task.

For instance, suppose that you are helping a student with English homework and that he has to read a ten-page short story. Instead of making him read all ten pages at once, have him read five pages and then go to a different activity, such as discussing what he has read, predict how the story will end, or have him act the story out. Then have the student finish reading the story later in the day.

Varying the Methods of Instruction

Another strategy that you could use to increase attention is to vary your method of instruction. Ever have a professor who just lectured? Isn't it boring? Students with ADHD probably feel the same way. Use a different method of instruction every ten to fifteen minutes.

For example, suppose you were teaching a social studies or history unit on the Vikings. Instead of presenting all of the information via a lecture or a film strip, have them find Scandinavia on globe, measure the distance between Norway and the coast of North America, brainstorm ideas as to why the Vikings wanted to go to North America, and share their ideas with the class. Perhaps they could compare the climates of Scandinavia and North America. Information can be taught in many diverse ways. If you vary your methods and have quick, yet structured, movement from activity to activity, you become a more dynamic teacher and are likely to hold the students' attention.

Using Technology

Nowadays, nearly every classroom and library has access to a personal computer. Many homes have them as well. Computers provide a multimedia presentation that can be a perfect teaching tool for students with attention deficits. Think about it. Computers have sound, colorful images that move, and are interactive. Using such technology not only keeps students' attention but also teaches them valuable academic skills. For example, there are computer "games" that teach students about the Civil War, such as who the key leaders are, what military strategies were used, and where famous battles were fought. Remember, learning can—and should be—fun.

Using Manipulatives

Another way of holding a student's attention is to plan hands-on activities. These activities often involve manipulatives, that is, representations of abstract concepts that the student can physically alter. For example, when teaching a student to tie her shoes, do you just tell her about it? Probably not. You have her practice actually tying her own shoe.

Same thing with learning math. Rather than just writing "2 + 2" on the board, give students blocks or marbles or anything that they can touch and count. This strategy can be used with any subject, as well as used at home.

Using Advanced Organizers

Another strategy for helping inattentive students is to use advanced organizers. In other words, map out or outline what is going to be covered in class so that the students have a better idea what information will be important and what information is just "setting the stage." A good way of doing this is to list all of the objectives for the lesson on the board. Before you begin the lesson, review the objectives, thus letting the students know what your expectations are. Further, as you begin to cover an objective while you are teaching, place a check by it on the board, thus letting the students see what you are discussing and what topic will come next. Finally, when you are finished with the lesson, review with the class what was accomplished. This will give them a clear summary of what was discussed and help them recall information later in the semester.

Study Guides

Much like advanced organizers, students often benefit from the use of study guides. Such guides help students focus their attention on the relevant information and away from extraneous material. Another variation of this strategy would be to have students develop their own study guide with your guidance. For example, before students begin to read a chapter in their textbook, have them glance through what they are supposed to read. Have them look at the pictures, tables, graphs, and subject headings. Then have them write down five or six questions that they think will be covered in the chapter. As they read, have them actively trying to answer their questions, much like they do when you create a study guide for them.

Lists of Assignments

There are several strategies that you could use to help students who frequently lose or forget things. For instance, with homework, have a list on door of all the assignments that are due the next day. Draw the students' attention to the list every day before they leave. Before they leave for home or school, have them check to make sure that they have all of the materials that they will need.

Day Planners and Notebooks

Another strategy would be to have each student keep a day planner or notebook. In it, they should write down what they have to do, what they need in order to do it, and when it has to be done. The trick is getting the student in the habit of writing things down and checking the notebook on a regular basis. You can help facilitate this habit by making students write things in the notebook during the last five minutes of every class period. Further, having the student keep the notebook in the same place (e.g., in their backpack) will help prevent it from getting lost.

One way of modifying this strategy for home is to have parents keep a list of chores on the refrigerator door. After completing a task, the student can check it off. This not only helps the parents see their child's progress but also prompts the student to see what else he has left to do.

Partial Assignments

When students have difficulty maintaining their attention, they often miss details and make careless mistakes on their homework. For example, suppose that you have a student who gets the first ten math problems correct, but misses all the rest. What should you do?

You could have her do every third problem. Further, you can arrange it so that, if she gets at least 90 percent of the problems correct, she gets a reward (e.g., extra playtime, etc.). However, if she doesn't get at least 70 percent of the problems correct, she has to do another set of problems until she does.

This strategy can be applied to any subject. For example, if your student gets 90 percent or above on his spelling pretest, he doesn't have to take the posttest. The key, however, is to make sure your student does enough work so that you know he understands the material. Don't allow students to get away with a shoddy education.

Peer Teaching

Another way of helping students make sure they don't forget things or make careless mistakes is to use "peer teaching" or "peer coaching." One method of doing this is to have students work in pairs. Each student helps their partner remember to do homework and other activities. You could even have a competition where the "team" who turns in the most homework gets a snack or bonus points.

Problems can arise when the study partner becomes more of a distraction than an asset. For example, during adolescence, placing male and female students together might create a situation that diverts attention away from the activity. Further, you might accidentally pair two students who don't like each other, thus creating conflict, or two students who "feed off" of each other's behavior, such as making inappropriate comments back and forth. Take care when pairing students.

WHAT SKILLS ARE NEEDED TO IMPROVE INATTENTION?

Let's suppose that you modified your student's environments (e.g., school and home) and both the student's parents and teachers are utilizing multiple teaching strategies. Are you finished working with the student? Nope, not by a long shot.

Think of it this way. Suppose that after adopting new teaching strategies and changing the environment, everything is fine. The student now pays attention and is learning math, science, and all the other subject areas. What is going to happen next year when he has a different teacher? Things are likely to revert to the way they were. That is why students need to learn skills that they can use when teachers and parents are no longer around. There are many ways of doing this.

Prioritizing

When using lists to help students remember tasks, it is also helpful to teach students how to prioritize. Think for a moment of all of the things that you have to do this week—all of the household chores, social activities, and work. If you made yourself focus on all of those activities, you would probably feel a bit overwhelmed. So too would students with ADHD. Having them develop lists of what they have to do might put a lot of pressure on them. Teaching them how to prioritize might prevent unneeded stress.

When teaching students how to prioritize, you could have students focus on a number of variables. For example, you can have them complete the tasks that are due the soonest, focus on tasks that are worth the most points, or complete tasks that are required versus those that are optional. The idea here is to help students develop some sort of formula by which they can decide which assignment to complete first.

Taking Notes

A strategy that can be used both at school and at home is taking notes. You are probably thinking that this strategy is self-evident and obvious, but how many students really know how to take good notes? Do you remember when you were in school and you had a teacher who lectured every period? The teacher just kept putting up overhead after overhead and you copied them as fast as you could, or you tried to write down every word that the professor said. Then, when it was time to study for the big test, you looked at your notes only to realize that you couldn't understand them! They were just scribblings of phrases with no context or main idea. Chances are, the notes of students with ADHD are just like that. If you don't think so, ask them for their notes and see for yourself.

Good note taking is a skill that is learned. That means somebody has to teach students how to do it properly. That person is you.

One of the most important skills that you need to teach students is to identify the main topic of a discussion and its supporting points. Developing this skill takes time, experience, and guidance. One way students can develop this skill is for them to examine the notes of their teachers. This way they can see how notes are structured and what information is important to write down. Further, students can use their teachers' notes as an advanced organizer. You can also allow students to use their notes on exams or quizzes. This will give them incentive to learn how to take notes effectively.

Metacognition

Another strategy to help inattentive students is to have them think about their own thinking, which is called "metacognition." The idea is to have students self-monitoring their behavior. For instance, every few minutes a student might ask herself, "Was I paying attention to what I was supposed to?" The student might even keep track of how frequently she was paying attention to the teacher versus other stimuli.

This strategy has advantages and disadvantages. First, since it is a student-driven intervention, it will not take much of your time. You might have to get the student used to thinking about her own thought processes, but the student completes the actual recording. Second, the strategy can be used anyplace. For example, when older students are driving, they can think to themselves, "Am I keeping my mind on where I am going?"

The downside of having students reflect on their own thought processes is that it might divert their attention. For example, suppose that as you are reading this book, somebody walks up to you and asks, "What are you reading?" You mark your place and tell them. When you try to return to reading, you find that you are no longer in the mood.

The same thing can happen with your students. Suppose that they are paying attention to every word that you are saying. However, when they ask themselves, "Am I focusing on what I should be focusing on?" they are no longer paying attention to you. Still, if used properly, metacognition strategies can help a student regulate their own behavior.

One way to help students get into the habit of monitoring their behavior is to have teachers and parents use a simple gesture as a reminder. For example, if you are teaching and you see that your student is apparently daydreaming, you could tap your index and thumb fingers together. That will cue your student to reflect on their thinking. Further, the subtle movement of tapping your fingers is not distracting to other students nor should it take you off task.

APPLYING WHAT YOU HAVE LEARNED

Before teaching students who are inattentive, you must first answer many questions. Consider for a moment the case study of Stacey at the beginning of the chapter. Do you think she has ADHD? What are some of the other possibilities that might explain her behavior? How would you modify her environments to help her pay attention? What strategies would you suggest her teachers use to help her pay attention? Finally, what skills would you teach Stacey so that she can be better able to pay attention when teachers aren't present?

Does Stacey Have ADHD?

What is your assessment? Do you think that Stacey has ADHD? If so, what type?

Three things are clear in Stacey's case study. First, she is having difficulties that are substantially and adversely affecting her life. Specifically, she is failing at school and not developing friendships. Second, these difficulties appear to be consistent through multiple environments. Remember, her parents said that she is "strange" at home. Plus, Stacey is not paying attention in most of her classes. Finally, she exhibits enough behaviors that might justify a diagnosis of ADHD-I, or ADHD Predominantly Inattentive. For example, she is forgetful, often loses things, often has difficulty organizing her thoughts, has difficulty sustaining attention, fails to complete homework, and fails to pay attention to detail.

The questions that remain are, "Was Stacey this way when she was younger?" Or is this new behavior for her? If she has always been inattentive, she is likely to have ADHD-I. However, if her behavior is recent, other factors are more likely at play.

What Other Possibilities Explain Stacey's Behavior?

Stacey obviously has serious concerns that need to be addressed, but are these concerns the result of ADHD-I or something else? What other explanations can you think of that might be causing Stacey's situation?

One obvious possibility is depression. Stacey appears to be withdrawn and isolated. Further, depression could explain the lack of interest in school and poor attention. If you suspect depression, get Stacey help immediately!

Another explanation could be drugs. Certainly, if Stacey is abusing alcohol or marijuana, she will appear to be "spacey" and incoherent. If her behavior is recent, rather than lifelong, the possibilities of drugs and depression are the prime suspects.

Finally, Stacey may be having problems at home. Just because her parents are affluent and appear to be interested in her education doesn't mean that they are above child abuse. Perhaps Stacey isn't getting the attention she needs from her family.

You may never know what is causing Stacey's difficulties, but with more information and some good guesswork, you could reduce the number of possibilities. Once you have selected the most likely cause for the problem, you will need to begin to address the problem.

How Would You Change Stacey's Environments?

Environmental factors often contribute to a student's inability to pay attention. This makes sense. Could you be reading this text if the light were too dim, or if there were a train going by your window? For this reason, you must examine the environments in which your students have difficulty paying attention. With this in mind, what would you do in Stacey's case?

For starters, you might want to move Stacey away from the window. This could reduce the stimuli that are distracting her. Secondly, she might feel intimidated by the people who sit around her, so try having her sit next to some supportive peers. Maybe this would help her make friends. Finally, if she is losing her homework and books, perhaps her parents could organize her bedroom or home study area.

What Strategies Would You Use to Teach Stacey?

Changing the environment will only help so much. You'll have to examine the strategies that have been used to teach students who are displaying attention problems. After all, the quality of teaching often will dictate the quality of students' learning. What kind of strategies would you use with Stacey?

First of all, teachers probably shouldn't use a lot of lecturing. It is natural for students to have difficulty paying attention when they are being talked at, so try to use more active learning, such as group activities. Further, group activities may help Stacey develop positive friendships with her peers. You might also want to use hands-on activities. For example, if Stacey is having difficulty focusing her attention during math, use manipulatives rather than worksheets or problems on the board. What other strategies could you use?

What Skills Would You Teach Stacey?

It is not enough for you to get students to pay attention during school or when other people are prompting them. What is going to happen when they are no longer in school? How are they going to succeed if they can't focus their attention? This is why students need to learn skills that they could use throughout their lives. With this in mind, what skills would you teach Stacey?

For example, you might want to teach Stacey to jot down a few notes before answering questions in order to help organize and guide her responses. Notes, such as what chores she has to do and when, could also help her at home. You might also teach her how to socialize effectively and how to advocate for herself when other people are giving her a hard time.

CHAPTER 3

Methods of Addressing Impulsivity

CHAPTER OBJECTIVES

This chapter answers the following questions:

1. How can impulsivity be a problem?
2. How can the environment affect impulsivity?
3. How can teaching strategies affect impulsivity?
4. What skills are needed to reduce impulsivity?

CASE STUDY: ROBERT

What can I say about Robert? At first glance, he is a typical second grader—bright, energetic, and full of questions, but after watching him in class or on the playground for two minutes, anybody can see that he is very different from the other students.

Robert has great difficulty following directions and conforming to classroom rules. For example, he rarely, if ever, raises his hand when asking or answering a question. He just yells what he has to say across the room. Further, he frequently blurts out comments that are so bizarre, I often wonder if he is clinically insane. Such as once, during science time, the class was discussing the difference between plants and animals. Out of the blue, Robert felt it necessary to run around the room singing, "I can fly! I can fly!" On another occasion, during church, he apparently announced, very loudly to the congregation, "My dog licks his pee-pee." Needless to say, he can be a huge disruption wherever he goes.

Additionally, not a day has gone by this semester when he hasn't gotten in trouble for touching other students or their belongings. I wouldn't say that he steals things, but he does have a tendency of borrowing other people's property without asking permission. Moreover, if he wants to see something that somebody else has, Robert will just grab it away from the other student. As a result, few students play with him during recess or eat with him during lunch.

His mother and I have tried numerous forms of punishment to rectify Robert's behavior. For example, I didn't let him go to recess for nearly two weeks, thinking that this would compel him to stop yelling inappropriate comments in class—but it did not work. I also used time-out where he sat by himself in the hallway, but he wanders away from the time-out desk and gets into trouble.

I want to get Robert medicated, but his mother is resistant. He definitely needs something.

Case Study Questions

1. Do you think that Robert has ADHD? Explain.
2. What other conditions could account for Robert's behavior?
3. How could you change the environment to lessen Robert's impulsivity?
4. What teaching strategies would you use to lessen Robert's impulsivity?
5. What skills would you teach Robert to lessen his impulsivity?

HOW CAN IMPULSIVITY BE A PROBLEM?

Impulsivity can have a major impact on the lives—the academics, social life, and safety within the community—of students with ADHD. Imagine you are taking the SAT or ACT. You quickly read the questions and then selected the first option that sounded plausible without considering any other potential answers. Do you think you would do well on the test?

Imagine that you are at a party and you see somebody that you would like to get to know. You walk up to her or him to initiate a conversation. What you want to say is "Hi, my name is Rob. What is yours?" but instead you hear yourself saying "Nice butt." What kind of impression do you think you made? Do you think the other person has an accurate assessment of who you are?

One more creative visualization: Imagine that you are driving to work or school and you suddenly notice that the left-hand lane is moving quicker than the lane you are in. Suddenly, as if on its own, your car swings into the left-hand lane before you can check to see if it is clear. How many accidents do you think you would get into throughout your life? Could you afford your car insurance, or to keep fixing your car? What if you seriously hurt somebody? Would your life be different than it is now?

All of these examples illustrate what life is like for many people with ADHD-HI or ADHD-C. For example, they do things without taking the time to think them through, such as answering questions quickly or driving erratically. They tend to rush through activities and make careless mistakes, much like students who are inattentive. Further, they say things without regard to other people's feelings. In fact, many times they will make comments but not realize that they said them aloud. In addition to saying exactly what is on their minds, people who are impulsive might also start fights, make unwanted physical contact with other people, and exhibit behaviors that others might consider bizarre.

People who are impulsive are free thinkers. They tend to be immensely creative. They often perceive the world in very unique ways and are able to develop solutions to very complex problems. However, in order for students to make their impulsivity a gift, they must be taught how to harness and control their impulses. To do this, you will need to optimize the environment, enhance your teaching, and give the students skills.

HOW CAN THE ENVIRONMENT AFFECT IMPULSIVITY?

Many of the problems caused by impulsivity are related to the environment. For example, ever watch students with ADHD repeatedly poking or annoying other students when they were supposed to be doing seatwork? It is almost as if students with ADHD can't help themselves. They get a thought in their head and they have to act on it. Modifying the environment may help deter this behavior before it starts.

Increasing the Distance between Desks

When modifying the environment, you may wish to begin by examining the student's immediate surroundings. How much distance is there between the student and his peers? Try giving the impulsive student enough personal space so that no other students are in reach. However, take care not to give the student so much space that it looks as if he is being punished or isolated.

Personal space can also be a factor in other environments as well. For example, if a child is having trouble sitting at the dinner table or during church without bothering his or her siblings, try increasing the space between them. If additional space isn't available, try having the child sit between two adults.

Taking Away Tempting Targets

In addition to removing impulsive students from tempting situations, you could also remove tempting situations from the student. For example, suppose that a student constantly grabs markers from the teacher's desk. A very simple way of preventing him from writing all over everything is to put the markers in a drawer. Ever hear of the expression, "Out of sight, out of mind"?

This is a very useful strategy for preventing inappropriate behaviors at school and at home. It is particularly important when the student's impulsivity can lead to injury or property damage. For example, if a student acts inappropriately with scissors or tools, putting these implements in a locked cabinet helps reduce the risk of accidents. Also, parents with valuables, such as antiques or priceless knickknacks, could prevent damage by placing them in rooms not frequented by their children (e.g., the master bedroom or study).

Giving the Student Only What Is Needed

Frequently, when students are inundated with objects, they feel compelled to get rid of them in inappropriate ways. For example, a student with an entire desk full of pencils might try to throw the pencils into the air so that they stick into the ceiling. If you make sure that the student only has what is needed to complete an assignment, the chance that she will abuse the excess objects is reduced.

List of Rules

Making students aware of the rules is imperative for effective teaching, both at home and school. Further, students who are impulsive frequently need reminders. One way to remind students about the rules without interrupting your teaching or without drawing attention to the student's inappropriate behavior is to have the rules laminated and attached to the top of the student's desk or on the bedroom door. This will give the student a constant visual reminder as to what behavior is expected.

HOW CAN TEACHING STRATEGIES AFFECT IMPULSIVITY?

If a student is so engrossed in what you are teaching, you are likely to lessen the potential for disruptive behavior. It is therefore important to use teaching strategies that not only prevent possible inappropriate behavior but also minimize the effects of the impulsive behaviors that do occur. There are several methods of enhancing your teaching to produce these results.

Choosing Your Battles

One of the keys to being an effective teacher or parent is to take great care when choosing your battles. This is true with all children. Imagine that your parents and teachers corrected you every time that you made a mistake. Suppose that every time you opened your mouth, they corrected your grammar or told you a better way of saying something. How would you feel? Would you speak a lot in class or tell your parents what you did over the weekend? Chances are, after a while, you will begin to feel "beaten down." This is just how students with ADHD would feel if you tried to correct everything that they say or do that is wrong.

Before you begin teaching, you need to have a clear understanding of what types of behavior you will and will not tolerate. For example, what if a student called you by your first name? Is that something that you would correct? Would you correct the student every time? Some of the time? Not at all? How about if your students used "mild" profanity, such as "shit" or "damn"? What if they use this language after falling down and hurting themselves? Would that matter to you? When can students be out of their seats? Should a student ask permission to sharpen a pencil? These are only some of the situations in which you will find yourself. Knowing how you will handle them before they occur will help you select which behaviors you want to discipline and which you will ignore.

But choosing your battles is not enough; you have to choose them consistently. Imagine if you had a teacher who sometimes let you ask questions without raising your hand, but yelled at you for the same thing at other times. You probably would be pretty confused and reluctant to say anything at all. In other words, as a parent or educator, consistency is everything!

Behavioral Contracts

Behavioral contracts can help with most behavior problems. The idea is to sit down with the student and to negotiate consequences for certain behaviors. For instance, if the student goes a week without getting into a fight, he gets extra playtime. If he gets into a fight, however, he cannot play in that week's Little League game.

The key to behavioral contracts is that both sides must agree to the outcomes. Students, parents, and teachers must all be involved with the process. Further, behaviors must be clearly defined so that there is no argument as to whether the contract has been fulfilled or violated.

An interesting twist to this strategy is to have a third-party mediator aid in the development of the contract. A neutral perspective might defuse hostilities between you and the student, or between the student and the parents. You could also have a mock trial if a dispute arises regarding the contract. However, if you use a mock trial, you must be willing to accept the verdict of the jury, which could be comprised of other students and adults.

Guide during Transitions

Lack of structure is the bane of most impulsive students. When there is chaos, there is likely to be trouble. Times of chaos usually involve transition, that is, going from one activity to another. For example, students waiting for class to begin are often not supervised. The same is true for most activities at home. As a result, inappropriate behavior is likely to transpire.

To prevent difficulties during transition, teachers and parents need to provide structure. For instance, you could provide "two-minute warnings" before starting new activities. This gives students an opportunity to adjust and prepare for a different set of expectations.

Try to think of things from the perspective of students with ADHD. You have been cooped up in a classroom or house for several hours, trying to follow the rules and behave yourself. Finally, it is time to go to recess or play outside where you can blow off a little steam and not think of all of the rules. Then, all of a sudden, you are back in class or the house again. Can you imagine how hard it is for an impulsive student to keep adjusting to different situations? These students can't turn their impulsivity on and off like a light. They need time and support. By letting students know that there are a couple minutes left during recess or playtime, you are giving them time to settle down and focus on the rules of the next situation.

WHAT SKILLS ARE NEEDED TO REDUCE IMPULSIVITY?

To function well in society, students with ADHD need to possess certain skills. For example, they have to think things through before they act and they have to restrain themselves from saying whatever comes to mind. In short, students have to learn to control their impulses. There are several ways of teaching this skill at school and at home.

Develop Wait Time

One of the most important skills that impulsive students can develop is "wait time." For example, many impulsive students will rush through an assignment and then turn it in right away even if they do not know some of the answers. If they learn to set the assignment aside for a few minutes before turning it in, they may remember the answers that eluded them earlier.

Double-Checking Work

Remember in math class how the teacher always told you to double-check your work? Did you? For impulsive students who tend to make careless mistakes, double-checking their work can mean the difference between showing their true potential and failing miserably. Getting them into the habit of double-checking their work, however, might be a challenge. As with any acquired habit, it takes repetition. One way of providing this repetition is to have students verbally check their work with you. Another way is to have students "grade" their work; if they get a problem wrong, they have to determine where the error began as well as how to correct it.

Self-Monitoring

Self-monitoring is a primary component of any behavioral modification program. Simply put, your student monitors his own behavior in an attempt to behave appropriately. Strategies for self-monitoring include having your student think to himself "Am I behaving like I should?" You could also have a checklist on your student's desk that outlines your expectations for good behavior (e.g., raising a hand before blurting out the answer, keeping hands to yourself, etc.). The student can then refer to the checklist at designated points of the day to see if he is complying with the classroom rules.

This strategy can be used at home as well. The student can have a list on his bedroom door reminding him to pick up after himself, to do his chores, and not to run in the house. Additionally, instead of yelling, the parents can redirect their child by merely saying, "Check your behavior." At this point, the student is to stop what he is doing and reflect upon his behavior, comparing his behavior to what is expected of him.

Practice Appropriate Behavior

Behavior is learned. Typically, we emulate behavior that is modeled around us. It is therefore important to make sure impulsive students have positive examples of how to behave. You might have students role-play situations that give the impulsive student difficulty. For example, you could have students act out the appropriate way of dealing with a disagreement on the playground. You could also have students act out inappropriate behaviors and then discuss why the behavior was inappropriate. Finally, you should be an example of expected behavior. From time to time, you might want to explain to the student why you behaved a certain way and how you determined what the correct way to act was.

Turn Impulsivity into a Positive

All too often, teachers and parents try to make students perfect while forgetting that some degree of impulsivity is fun and even necessary. Your goal should be to give students the ability to learn, socialize, and develop the kind of life that they want to live. You should not try to make them something that they are not or deprive them of who they are.

With this in mind, it important to have students use their natural gifts in positive ways. Impulsive students tend to be creative and funny.

They tend to be the class clowns. Even though all the world loves a clown, you may need to teach students when it is appropriate to be funny and when it is expected that they be serious.

In order to help students with ADHD, teachers and parents need to understand that, in and of itself, impulsivity is not a bad thing. If harnessed and utilized legitimately, it can be a gift. Think for a moment of a time when you had to work with a group of classmates. Perhaps you had to work on a difficult project. Who better to have on your team than somebody who was creative and viewed the problem in a different light?

In addition to having students monitor their own behavior, try to monitor yours. How many negative things do you say to your impulsive student? How many positive things do you say? For every time that you tell your student something negative, try to tell them three positive things. In essence, you are reminding them that they have worth.

APPLYING WHAT YOU HAVE LEARNED

Impulsive students present teachers and parents with many challenges. Impulsivity, however, can be a good thing. Students who are impulsive can be creative, energetic, and good spirited. Your goal should be to give students the skills that they need to succeed in life, not to make them into different people.

Helping impulsive students to learn, fit in socially, and follow rules is part of your job as a teacher or parent. Although this may appear to be a daunting task, you may be more successful if you address three areas. The first is to modify the student's environment so that you minimize the temptation to act inappropriately. The second is to enhance your teaching so that you can redirect students before they break your rules. The third is to teach the student skills that can be used outside the classroom and later in life.

Reread the case study of Robert in the beginning of the chapter. Do you think he has ADHD? What else could explain his behavior? How would you change his environments? What teaching strategies should his parents and teachers use? What skills would you teach him?

Does Robert Have ADHD?

If Robert were your student or child, would you diagnose him with ADHD? If so, what type? Let's look at the available information.

First of all, Robert appears to have enough symptoms to be diagnosed with ADHD-HI. Specifically, he leaves his seat, runs around, has difficulty being quiet, talks excessively, blurts out answers, and has difficulty waiting. Second, Robert's difficulties appear to be adversely affecting his educational and social development to a significant degree. Third, Robert exhibits symptoms in numerous environments, including his classroom, recess, and church. Finally, Robert's difficulties are present by age seven as required by APA's definition of ADHD. Although additional information should be gathered, a diagnosis of ADHD-HI might be appropriate for Robert.

What Else Could Be Causing Robert's Behavior?

Even though it appears that a diagnosis of ADHD-HI is appropriate for Robert, there might be other explanations for his behavior. Can you think of any?

One possible explanation for Robert's behavior is that he is just a rowdy child. Perhaps he is an only child and he is not use to sharing with others. Further, maybe his parents do not discipline him effectively and he has become a spoiled brat. How could you find out if these options are plausible?

Another explanation is that Robert has a conduct disorder. Conduct disorders are characterized by a willful disregard for rules and socially acceptable behavior. As indicated in chapter 1, students with ADHD tend to also have conduct disorders. How would you determine if Robert has ADHD-HI or a conduct disorder? Or both?

How Would You Change Robert's Environments?

Can you think of some ways that the environment is contributing to Robert's behavior? How about when he touches other students? How could you change his environments in order to decrease this behavior?

One way is to put more distance between Robert and his peers. Perhaps you could suggest to the teacher that he rearrange the room so that Robert's desk is not too close to other students. You could even have him sit closer to the front of the room where the teacher can keep an eye on him.

How about when he takes things without permission? How could you minimize this behavior by changing the environment? You could try making sure everything is put away, especially things that he might be tempted to take or play with.

What Strategies Would You Use to Teach Robert?

It appears obvious that punishment has no effect on Robert's behavior, so you might want to try a reinforcement program. For example, if Robert raises his hand before speaking, he gets a check mark. If he gets five check marks before lunch, he may use the computer to play an educational game; if Robert refrains from taking things that don't belong to him, he is praised and allowed ten extra minutes of recess.

What Skills Would You Teach Robert?

Can you imagine what Robert would be like as an adult if he doesn't change his behavior? Do you think he will be able to obtain and maintain a job? Develop lasting friendships? What skills would you teach Robert so that he could succeed in life?

Self-monitoring might be a good thing for Robert to learn, especially regarding social skills. His parents and teachers can help him monitor his behavior by frequently asking him "What is appropriate behavior in this situation?" Robert is to then model appropriate behavior, such as raising his hand or asking permission to borrow an object. Self-monitoring could also help Robert think before he says something.

CHAPTER 4

Methods of Addressing Hyperactivity

CHAPTER OBJECTIVES

This chapter answers the following questions:

1. How can hyperactivity be a problem?
2. How can the environment affect hyperactivity?
3. How can teaching strategies affect hyperactivity?
4. What skills are needed to improve hyperactivity?

CASE STUDY: FREYA

I teach in a middle school gifted program. I have a couple students in my program who are not only gifted but also have various disabilities, such as hearing impairments and learning disorders, so I have some experience with kids who have special needs. Unfortunately, I have a student named Freya who is baffling me and the rest of the staff.

Freya is a twelve-year-old eighth grader who has skipped the second and fourth grades. She has a full-scale IQ of 143, reads at the college level, and can do advanced math that I can't even understand. She is personable, highly energetic, and immensely driven to succeed. Not only does she participate in numerous academic clubs, but she is also on the swimming, gymnastics, tennis, and girls' softball teams. In general, she is a great kid.

Although she is gifted intellectually, Freya fails most of her tests and quizzes, which causes her great frustration. Her other teachers and I know that she understands the material and can do much better. It is just that she makes careless mistakes and leaves many questions unanswered.

Freya also tends to be immensely impatient. She will tap her pencil on her desk and will tell her teachers to "hurry up" if we are spending too much time on a topic that she already knows. She is like this socially as well. I frequently hear Freya tell her friends, "Get to the point" when they are talking to her.

I have spoken with Freya's parents and previous teachers. They all have noted similar behaviors. Freya's father feels that her poor test grades and social skills are the result of being bored by the material and people around her. He believes Freya should be promoted to high school where she can experience greater challenges.

I, however, feel that if Freya doesn't learn to take tests she will never do well in college. In fact, if she doesn't do well on the SAT or ACT, she probably will not get into a top school. Further, Freya needs to be able to relate to people who are not on her intellectual plane. However, I have no idea how to teach her these things.

Case Study Questions

1. Do you think that Freya has ADHD? Explain.
2. What other conditions could account for Freya's behavior?
3. How could you change the environment to lessen Freya's hyperactivity?
4. What teaching strategies would you use to lessen Freya's hyperactivity?
5. What skills would you teach Freya to lessen her hyperactivity?

HOW CAN HYPERACTIVITY BE A PROBLEM?

Children who are hyperactive will probably demand more of your time than children who are inattentive and staring off into space. They are hard to ignore and difficult to control. Further, hyperactive students tend to have multiple issues. Not only do they display large amounts of energy, they can also have difficulty paying attention and socializing.

Imagine that you have a child who has ADHD-HI. What do you suppose her behavior would be like? She probably is constantly moving. Even when she is in her seat, some part of her body is in motion. Perhaps she is tapping her finger or bouncing her knee or fidgeting in her chair. She probably stands up for no apparent reason and walks around the room. When you talk with her, you get the impression that she isn't focused solely on you. Further, she tends to talk excessively with sentences that seem to run together with no common theme.

As you are trying to develop ways of teaching this student, you must keep three very important things in mind. First, students who are hyperactive have difficulty controlling themselves much like students who are impulsive. You cannot just tell hyperactive students to sit still and expect them to be able to do it. Their condition is physiological. For whatever reason, their bodies have a need to expend energy. They can't turn it on or off on cue.

Think of hyperactivity as an itch. If you concentrate hard enough, you can force yourself not to scratch. However, while you are concentrating, it is difficult to attend to anything else, such as a teacher or parent. Moreover, much like scratching, hyperactive children will eventually have to expel their pent-up energy. The trick is to have them expel their energy in positive, productive ways.

Second, students with ADHD-C or -HI are not always hyperactive. In fact, hyperactivity frequently goes in cycles. Sometimes your students will be so hyperactive they will be unable to focus their attention long enough to read a sentence; other times they will be able sit and watch television or play a video game for hours on end. Understanding and utilizing cycles will help you to teach and your students to learn.

Third, much like impulsivity, hyperactivity can be a gift. Students with hyperactivity, by definition, have incredible amounts of energy. If they are able to harness this energy and use it appropriately, they can accomplish great feats in very short periods of time. Below are some ways that teachers and parents can help students channel their hyperactivity productively.

HOW CAN THE ENVIRONMENT AFFECT HYPERACTIVITY?

Have you ever been in a room that was so crowded and noisy that you felt claustrophobic? Were you overpowered by an incredible urge to leave the room? That is close to what hyperactive individuals feel like when they are experiencing a hyperactive phase. They don't necessarily feel claustrophobic, but they have this driving need to move, whether it is to leave the room or to fidget in their chair or talk excessively. Like you in a crowded room, students' environments can influence their hyperactivity. Therefore, in order to help your students learn, you should examine their environments, both at school and home, and make modifications that might improve their functioning.

Create a Calm Classroom

In order for you to teach any student, his or her environment must be conducive to learning. To teach hyperactive students, places of learning will need to be calming and relaxing. There are several ways to create a relaxing environment. For example, you could use soft background music, or sounds of the ocean or rain forest. You could also replace florescent lights with less harsh "full-spectrum" lighting. Fish tanks, lava lamps, and plants also have been found to reduce stress. Finally, consider painting the walls a relaxing color, such as light blue or hunter green.

Classroom Organization

Another method of creating a relaxing environment is to avoid clutter. The room should be well organized and devoid of piles of papers or books. Desks, tables, and other furniture should be arranged in such a way that they convey structure and not chaos. There should be enough room so that students will not feel claustrophobic.

These principles can be used at home as well. The student's bedroom should be relaxing and not overstimulating. Parents can develop a "quiet room" inside the house, some place where the student can unwind.

Have Two Desks

Another modification to classrooms is to give hyperactive students two desks. This has dual purposes. The first is that it gives students multiple places where they can work. This may be difficult for somebody who is not hyperactive to understand, but sometimes students need a change of view. If they are allowed to face a different direction or be in a different part of the room, they are better able to concentrate.

Secondly, having two desks enables a student to have one free from clutter. One desk can contain all of the student's supplies. The other will have a clear workspace.

Have an Activity Station with Manipulatives

An effective environment should also contain an "activity corner." This is the opposite of a quiet area where students can sit and read or do their homework. An activity corner is a place where hyperactive students can go when they are unable to sit down. For example, you can use a room divider to partition off a portion of the room. Here, out of view of the other students, hyperactive students can expel energy by playing educational games, using computers, or participating in active learning activities.

Altering the Classroom Setup

Hyperactive students get bored very easily with their surroundings. Pictures that they once liked no longer interest them. In the beginning of the year, they liked sitting in the back of the room, but now they hate it. And so on. This displeasure with their environment can often fuel their hyperactive behavior. One method of taking this fuel away is to rearrange the room. You don't have to move everything, but sometimes moving the desks into a different shape or moving the location of a study corner will keep the classroom environment fresh and stimulating.

Parents can also rearrange their child's bedroom, or wherever they study. Further, if you have the child plan where everything should go, this strategy could be a learning activity. For example, have the student draw a scale picture of her room, measure the furniture, determine where each piece should go, and then figure out in what order furniture should be moved.

HOW CAN TEACHING STRATEGIES AFFECT HYPERACTIVITY?

Have you ever had a group of students who barely stayed awake as you taught? It is difficult to get excited about teaching students who don't put any energy into their own education. With this in mind, hyperactivity can be utilized in positive ways. For example, imagine a classroom where everybody wanted to answer your questions or everybody wanted to express his or her ideas regarding the topic at hand.

Dynamic classrooms don't just occur magically; you have to cultivate them. You have to utilize teaching strategies that maximize appropriate behavior. You also have to use teaching strategies that minimize inappropriate behavior.

Allow Student to Stand while Working

Why is it so important for students to remain seated? Perhaps you feel that having a student stand might distract the other children, or maybe you feel that a student who is out of her seat is somehow undermining your authority. The truth is, there is nothing wrong with having your student out of her seat—if you take precautions.

When your hyperactive student is unable to remain seated, have her stand quietly by her desk. To prevent distracting other students, she could go to the back of the room where she would not block anybody's view of the board. She could even have a second desk in the back of the room just for that occasion. Additionally, there are drafting tables that are much higher than regular school desks. Using such a table, your student would be able to work effectively while standing. Allowing your student to work while standing will help reduce fidgeting and other distractions to other students. As long as the student is productive, why should he or she be made to sit?

Give Responsibility

A great way of working with hyperactive students is to give them responsibilities. For example, you could have them run errands, hand out worksheets, or collect assignments. Anything productive that will expend energy could be useful.

This strategy can be used at home as well. For instance, parents could have their hyperactive children be "in charge" of certain activities. For example, it could be the child's job to walk the dog or to take care of the garden. However, these activities should be seen as a reward and not a punishment. It is therefore very important to know what is rewarding to your students. Asking them what they like is a good way to begin (see chapter 9).

Allow Frequent Breaks

Making a hyperactive student sit down or work on assignments when he just can't focus his thoughts is counterproductive. If a student cannot work because he is experiencing a hyperactive period, he might as well take a break. This is true of all students. Are you reading this entire book all in one sitting? You probably have taken several breaks before you got to this page.

However, allowing frequent breaks can present two problems. First, more frequent breaks mean your students will have less exposure to the subject matters you are teaching. Second, students might begin to abuse the idea of taking breaks.

To minimize these problems, make sure your students know that they are expected to complete the same amount of work whether or not they take a break. Do not allow hyperactivity to become an excuse to avoid learning. Further, you could give students course notes to help them compensate for parts of the lesson that they miss.

WHAT SKILLS ARE NEEDED TO IMPROVE HYPERACTIVITY?

In order to use their energy appropriately, your students will have to learn certain skills. These skills include ways of minimizing their energy when trying to concentrate as well as how to channel their energy into productive tasks. There are several ways to develop these skills.

Expelling Energy

Ever sit next to someone at a movie theater who is bouncing her knees? Throughout the whole movie, the person's legs vibrate as if she has to go to the bathroom or is very anxious about something. How enjoyable was the film?

As you can imagine, your nonhyperactive students will be just as distracted by a student with ADHD-HI or ADHD-C as you were at the movie theater. However, as we discussed at the beginning of this chapter, hyperactive students have a physical need to expel energy. How then, can you allow your students to expend energy without distracting everybody around them?

One way is to have hyperactive students wiggle their toes. Try it. Wiggle your toes. Do you think you would be distracted if somebody next to you did that? Probably not. Having your students wiggle their toes when they are hyperactive allows them to dispel their energy with minimal distraction to others. Further, it is a strategy that can be used anywhere—including movie theaters.

Fiddling with Objects

Students who are hyperactive often have great difficulty waiting. They tend to blurt out answers, cut to the front of the line, and become irritable when things don't occur when they want them too. One way to reduce the anxiety of these students is to give them something to do while they wait. For example, give them something with which to fiddle, such as stress-reducing balls. People reduce their stress by rolling ceramic balls in their hands. Large marbles could also suffice. They can also fiddle with small toys.

Mind Games

Students can also play "mind games" to occupy themselves while waiting. For example, they could look at the people around them and imagine who they are and what they do for a living. This is a great way of encouraging students to use their creativity.

Another mind game is to identify nearby objects that begin with each letter of the alphabet, such as an automobile for A and bird for B. To make the game even more challenging, identify objects that end with each letter of the alphabet. For example, pizza for A and crumb for B. Everything can be made into some sort of game.

These types of mental games are great strategies for hyperactive students. It gives them something to focus on when they have nothing else to do. These strategies are particularly useful when waiting in the lunch line and being in the car on long trips with the family.

Knowing Yourself

It is very important for students to understand their own strengths and weaknesses. For example, students should know their primary learning style (e.g., visual learners). Further, students should understand when and where they study best. This is particularly important for students who are hyperactive.

Hyperactivity tends to go in cycles. Some students maybe better able to concentrate during the morning, while others work better at night. Knowing what time is best for your student to study might help avoid frustration as well as increase productivity.

Students should also know what calms them down and what motivates them to learn. Exercise is a very good way to calm down a hyperactive student. Running, swimming, or riding a bike might help your students burn the excess energy that is preventing them from learning effectively. A daily exercise regime could reduce the negative impact that hyperactivity may have on a student's life.

Additionally, motivators are vital when developing an education program. Think about yourself for a moment. What motivates you? When you have twenty pages to read for tomorrow, do you ever say to yourself, "If I read ten pages before dinner, I will go get some ice cream?" or "If I finish this chapter by noon, I'll go for a walk or watch some television?" These are motivators. Teach your students how to find their own motivators and how to set goals for themselves using things that they like as rewards.

Focus on Multiple Tasks

When students are in a hyperactive phase, they can maximize their energy by focusing upon multiple tasks. This strategy is particularly helpful if the multiple tasks are diverse in nature. For example, a hyperactive student can complete a few math problems, then move on to reading a page or two of their book for English, and then practice spelling for a few minutes, and return to math. It is like working out. Some people like to spend ten minutes on a bike, then Stairmaster, then treadmill, rather than spending thirty minutes on only one machine. The variety makes working out and learning easier. The key to this strategy is to make sure students complete each assignment.

Active Learning

An effective skill for all individuals is to actively process information. Simply put, students should do more than listen to somebody or read words on the page. They should put themselves into the subject. For example, as you read this text, you should be picturing your students or children and imagining yourself using some of these strategies. In short, you are actively participating in your learning.

When you are teaching your students social studies, encourage them to picture themselves during the time period. When they are learning math, have your students mentally apply the concepts to something that they care about. For example, when converting fractions to decimals, your students can be thinking about batting averages in baseball or money. Becoming an active learner is the first step that your students will take in becoming a lifelong learner. When your students are no longer in your classroom, you will still be teaching them.

Utilize Hyperactivity as a Gift

Imagine having near limitless energy. Imagine being able to run around all day and never get tired, or being able to complete every task ahead of schedule. You could complete all of your household chores and still have time to read for leisure. Would this help you in your day-to-day life?

What you have been imagining could be your students with ADHD. Hyperactivity, like impulsivity, can be a gift. However, you will need to give your students encouragement as well as the skills needed to harness their energy. Explain to them how they will benefit if they learn to use their gifts appropriately. Put it in terms that they understand and care about. For example, a hyperactive football player is likely to react quicker and have greater endurance than a football player without hyperactivity. A student who utilizes her hyperactivity will complete chores and homework quicker and have more time for other activities than nonhyperactive peers. It is their gift; you just have to help them unwrap it.

APPLYING WHAT YOU HAVE LEARNED

Students who are hyperactive will attract your attention far more than students who are inattentive. Consequently, it is easy to think of hyperactivity as a negative thing. After all, most parents and teachers would prefer having children who are staring quietly off into space than climbing over tables or running around the room. This is unfortunate because, if properly motivated and channeled, hyperactive students can excel in life, much like Freya from the case study at the beginning of the chapter.

Freya's situation is not uncommon. Many students who are gifted intellectually and athletically display symptoms of ADHD, such as hyperactivity. Sometimes, her energy level helps her, such as with athletics and her many activities; sometimes, it might be a detriment, such as when she takes a quiz or a test. Does this mean that she has ADHD? What other conditions could be causing her behavior? How could you change her environments so that she does better on tests and maximize the appropriate use of her energy? What teaching strategies would you use to utilize her hyperactivity? What skills would you teach her so that she could succeed in life?

Does Freya Have ADHD?

So what do you think? Does Freya have ADHD or not? This can be a tough diagnosis. Although she obviously has a great deal of energy, Freya doesn't have many of the classical symptoms of ADHD-HI, such as fidgeting in her seat or talking excessively. Or does she?

Often, hyperactivity in the classroom decreases if the student exercises regularly, which Freya is clearly doing. It might be that she would display more of the traditional symptoms of ADHD-HI if she weren't involved in so many sports. Further, not all individuals who are hyperactive talk continuously. Does she have ADHD-HI or not?

Well, Freya's behavior certainly gives you reasons for concern. She appears to be impulsive, impatient, interrupts others, hyperactive, and has difficulty waiting. Moreover, these behaviors have been present in multiple environments for several years. Most importantly, her energy level evidently is affecting her grades and social life. This is reason alone to gather additional information. Specifically, have Freya and her parents fill out behavior rating scales. If Freya reports feeling chronically restless, difficulty controlling her emotions, and feels as if she has only two speeds—"fast" and "stop," you may have enough to diagnose her with ADHD-HI.

What Else Could Be Causing Freya's Behavior?

Suppose that you have Freya complete several behavioral rating forms and self-assessments. However, she does not complain about any additional ADHD symptoms. She clearly is having difficulty, but it doesn't appear to be the result of ADHD. So what else could it be? Any ideas?

Perhaps Freya has text anxiety. Whenever she takes tests, she might feel very nervous about doing poorly. As a result, her mind isn't fully on her work, which leads to careless mistakes and unanswered questions.

As for her impatience and poor social skills, some people cannot tolerate being bored. They are bossy and say exactly what is on their minds—much like Freya. This explanation might sound rather simplistic, but it is a possibility. Not everybody who has a lot of energy has ADHD, just like not everybody who has ADHD is hyperactive.

How Could You Change Freya's Environments to Utilize Her Hyperactivity?

Whether or not Freya has ADHD-HI, she needs help focusing her energies on tests and quizzes. One method of doing this is to change Freya's environment.

You could have Freya take her tests in the hall or library where she cannot see her classmates. If she cannot see her peers, perhaps she will not feel compelled to work so fast. Being away from her peers might also help her relax and not feel pressured by how quickly her friends are finishing the exam.

You might also allow Freya to sit in a resource area of the classroom when she feels "bored" by the teacher. In other words, when Freya feels that she knows the material, she can go work on the computer instead of telling the teacher to hurry up. However, make it very clear that it is Freya's responsibility to learn the material that she might miss. Given her intelligence and motivation to learn, this strategy might give her the flexibility that she needs.

What Strategies Would You Use to Teach Freya?

Students who have ADHD, as well as those who are gifted, frequently need diverse methods of instruction. Hyperactive students especially are often unable to sit still through a long lecture. Consequently, you frequently will have to help develop innovative teaching strategies for these students.

What strategies would you use if you were Freya's teacher? One strategy that could be beneficial is not allowing Freya to turn in quizzes or tests right away. After she completes a test or quiz, have her set it aside. Have her work on something else for a half an hour or so and then have her double-check her assignment. This could help her catch careless mistakes and missed questions.

Freya would also benefit from hands-on, active learning. Perhaps peer teaching would be more effective and engaging than lecturing her. Further, instead of quizzes and tests, you could have her complete projects, reports, and experiments.

The number of strategies that you could use with Freya is limitless. If you run out of ideas, ask your students what they would like to do. Students like Freya tend to be very creative. Who knows what kind of innovative activities and strategies they could develop on their own?

What Skills Would You Teach Freya?

Suppose that Freya is one of your students or children. By the end of the school year, what skills would you want her to have learned? Take a moment to think about that. What, exactly, are you trying to teach her?

One thing that you might want to teach her is how to interact with other people. For example, if she is getting impatient with her friends, she will need to find a better way of dealing with it than saying, "Get to the point." Perhaps she could learn how to summarize conversations and help guide them to their conclusions.

Freya also could benefit from learning how to take tests. Specifically, she needs to develop a system with which she feels comfortable. For example, she has to get into the habit of taking her time, double-checking her work, and answering all of the questions.

CHAPTER 5

Methods of Addressing Social Skills

CHAPTER OBJECTIVES

This chapter answers the following questions:

1. How can inappropriate social skills be a problem?
2. How can the environment affect social skills?
3. How can teaching strategies affect social skills?
4. What skills are needed to improve social behavior?

CASE STUDY: RAYMOND

Raymond is a student of mine who can be described in one word: odd. He is a sixteen-year-old with average grades and intelligence as well as an excitable personality. However, in addition to being extremely distractible and overactive, he displays remarkably bizarre and socially inappropriate behavior, especially around women.

For example, Raymond has more than once "poked" a woman's breast with his finger and said in a loud voice, "Bong! Bong!" He also has a tendency of saying whatever is on his mind, such as "You could stand to lose a few pounds" or "If your nose wasn't so big, you would be very pretty."

Consequently, Raymond has very few friends. Further, the ones he does have are a bad influence. Specifically, they encourage Raymond to continue his eccentric behaviors, especially those that bother female students.

I scold Raymond nearly every day. Each time he tells me that he doesn't mean to do the things that he does. He says, "They just happen." I believe him, but this makes me even more worried. If he is so unable to control his actions, I am afraid that he might have a serious psychotic problem. I don't know what to do.

Case Study Questions

1. Do you think that Raymond has ADHD? Explain.
2. What other conditions could explain Raymond's behavior?
3. How could you change the environment to improve Raymond's behavior?
4. What strategies would you use to teach Raymond?
5. What skills would you teach Raymond?

HOW CAN INAPPROPRIATE SOCIAL SKILLS BE A PROBLEM?

Think about your life for a moment. Imagine that school is going well. You are learning a lot and will be able to pick any job that you desire. Your health is good. Everything couldn't get any better—except for the fact that you don't have any friends. Would you say that you have a good life?

Academics are important, but what would your life be like if you had no friends? Would you be motivated to go to school if you had nobody to sit with during lunch, or nobody with whom to play during recess? Unfortunately, one of the primary characteristics of ADHD is difficulty socializing.

Think about it. How likely are you to hang out with somebody who talked excessively, never seemed to pay attention to what you were saying, was emotionally immature, and behaved impulsively? Your answer is probably the same as those from the other students. As a result, children with ADHD are frequently lonely, isolated, and depressed.

For students with ADHD, developing healthy social relationships may be the difference between going to prison and living a happy life. Good relationships promote self-esteem. They also enable students to construct a "safety net" that will help prevent them from making disastrous choices. Think about your life and your friends for a moment. Have you ever gotten into a bad situation and your friends helped you see the way out? Perhaps they gave you the advice that you needed or helped you see things in a brighter light. Just as much as teachers and parents, friends can be important educators in the lives of your students.

Students need positive relationships with their peers. They also need them with their siblings and other family members. There are several ways that you can help students with ADHD cultivate these relationships.

HOW CAN THE ENVIRONMENT AFFECT SOCIAL SKILLS?

Suppose for a moment that you were a kid who moved to a new town in the middle of summer. Unfortunately, your new neighborhood didn't have any children your age. Do you think you would make lots of new friends? Probably not. You see, the environment plays a large role in the development of your social skills.

For example, suppose that your new teacher ruled his classroom with an iron fist. He made you sit in rows and you never worked in groups. You were not allowed to talk to the students around you. Do you think that you would make many friends in that class?

Group Desks to Facilitate Social Interactions

One way to modify classrooms so that they promote the development of social skills is to group students' desks. For example, instead of having students' desks in neat rows, have them facing each other in pairs or groups of fours. This will increase the likelihood of interaction between students. This type of classroom set-up, however, might create a noisier environment and make it more difficult for inattentive students to pay attention.

One modification to this strategy is to have "work stations" around the classroom. The students could have their desks in rows, but they work in groups during certain points of the day. This could produce opportunities for socialization, but give you more control as to when they occur.

Vary the Seating Chart

Another method for increasing social interactions is to periodically change the seating chart. This will give students opportunities to meet other students. For instance, have you ever sat in the same seat the entire school year? You probably knew the person in front of you, behind you, and to either side of you, but you probably didn't interact much with the students who sat across the room. Varying the seating chart will expose students with ADHD to potential new friends.

Limit Interactions with Negative Influences

You are probably thinking that if you vary your seating charts often, you will run the risk of having two "troublemakers" sitting next to each other. This is true. Promoting positive social skills sometimes means that you have to limit negative influences. For example, if there is a student in your class who likes to tease everybody and make fun of them, you should not place him by a shy student with no friends. Conversely, if you have a few students who are very friendly and willing to befriend other children, they might be the perfect "neighbors" for the student with ADHD.

Display Posters and Lists of Social Skills

One way of modifying both the classroom and the student's bedroom at home is to place posters on the walls that demonstrate appropriate social skills. The posters can also have key words or phrases to remind students of their goals. For example, a poster could say, "Discuss. Don't argue" or " Remember to say 'Thank You.'" Having parents and teachers refer to the posters periodically will help emphasize the importance of learning good social skills.

Remove Incentives to Limit Isolation

Another way that parents can encourage their children to develop social skills is to take away, or limit, incentives for being isolated. For example, if parents allow their children to view only one hour of television a night, the children will be forced to find something else to do with their time, such as playing with other kids. Further, parents can take away video games unless they are played with other children or only allow computers to be used for educational purposes.

HOW CAN TEACHING AFFECT SOCIAL SKILLS?

Changing the environment is a good step in helping your students develop social skills, but it is just the beginning. Now you will need to utilize teaching strategies that promote positive interactions.

Develop a Support Network

One way of assisting students in developing positive social relationships is to help them create a support network. In other words, help them make friends. Playing "matchmaker," however, can be difficult. Obvious attempts to create friendships can backfire, thus making the student feel even more worthless than before. For example, have you ever had friends try to set you up on a blind date? Did it make you feel as if you couldn't get a date on your own? Your students are likely to feel the same way.

Perhaps the easiest way to help students build friendships is to pair them up with other students on assignments. If you pair everybody up, it won't appear as if you are singling anybody out. Further, if you have a good idea what each student likes and dislikes, you could be more effective at pairing people who have similar interests.

You can also encourage students to join clubs and athletic teams at school. There are many opportunities for children to meet new friends in the community as well, such as softball leagues, 4-H, and church activities. All of these can help students meet peers who share similar interests and outlooks.

Provide Opportunities for Social Development

Another way to promote positive interactions is to provide structured opportunities for your students to interact. For example, you could break up the class into groups and have them work on projects. You could also have class debates or discussions about current topics. A very effective way for parents to provide opportunities for social interactions is to allow their children to throw parties or join sports teams or clubs.

Give Student Leadership Roles

Giving students opportunities to be leaders does three things. First, it forces students to communicate with other people. If you put a shy student or a student with ADHD in charge of a project, they will have to interact with the rest of their team. The key, however, is to monitor these interactions to make sure they are appropriate and positive, which we will discuss later.

The second outcome of giving your students opportunities to be leaders is that they have to develop and apply their critical thinking skills. They must analyze a task and determine how to work with people who do not always agree.

Finally, giving students opportunities to be leaders builds their confidence and self-esteem. Often students don't socialize because they are afraid or nervous to be around other people. Increasing their self-esteem is critical to promoting positive social development.

Provide Feedback

By itself, putting students into a leadership role won't always help them develop social skills. If a student is bossy and difficult to work with prior to being a leader, he or she will probably be bossy and difficult to work with when being a leader. While giving them experiences, you also have to give them opportunities to learn.

Your students need feedback. If they knew how to act appropriately, they probably would be doing so in the first place. Show them what they did right, what they did wrong, and what they did that needs some work. Using a video camera could be very useful with this process.

For example, when you put a student in charge of a project, videotape the group at work. Then, when the project is over, sit and watch some of the video with the student. Ask her what she thought she did well and what areas she could improve. Ask her what she would do differently if she were the project leader again. Give her strategies to communicate more effectively. Perhaps you could even have the rest of the group fill out evaluations of their leader. Further, make sure that all students have opportunities to be both leaders and followers. Sometimes the most effective leaders are those people who are experienced followers.

Have the Student Work with an Older Student

Have you ever noticed that people tend to model the behavior of the people around them? For example, if you go to a wild college bar with your friends, you might act wild and crazy. Yet, if you go to a classy restaurant with the same group of friends, you will probably act refined and dignified.

If you have students who are immature or act inappropriately, a great strategy to teach them social skills is to pair them up with an older, more responsible, student. High schools often have "cross-age programs" where high school students get credit for going to elementary or middle schools and tutoring students who need help. These programs can even be used for high school students by pairing freshmen and sophomores with upperclassmen, or upperclassmen with college students—such as pre-student teachers.

There are also community-based programs that pair students together. "Big Brother," "Big Sister," or "Buddies" are just three examples. If you don't have similar programs in your community, then perhaps you or the students' parents can start one with local churches or park districts.

Model Appropriate Interactions

In addition to older peers, your students model the behaviors of their teachers, parents, siblings, and—yes, even you. That is why it is important for you to model appropriate interactions. For example, ask somebody to role-play a disagreement in front of the student. You could even let the student believe the "fight" is real. Show students how two people can still get along even if they have different opinions.

Have your students' parents and family members model appropriate social skills. Perhaps they can make a point of having a conversation every night during dinner. They should encourage their children to join in and explain what they think about various topics. In this way, many people can model the behavior that students with ADHD are expected to display.

Teach Skills across Different Contexts

Social skills are used in nearly every environment imaginable—on the playground, in the classroom, on the bus to school, in the lunchroom, throughout the hallways, at the mall, at home, and in the community in general. As a result, you should teach social skills in numerous environments. For example, when developing a student's Individualized Education Plan (IEP), devise a way for a student to be rewarded for displaying positive social skills both at home and at the classroom. A student could receive anything from tokens to simple praise. You can even have the lunchroom monitor, bus driver, and playground supervisor be part of the plan. The idea is that students are being taught social skills in places other than just the classroom or home.

Schedule Quality Time

In order to develop a positive relationship, people need to spend time together. Without interactions, there are no relationships. With this in mind, it is often helpful for students to spend "quality time" with their family members. This time can be spent either as an entire family or one-on-one.

For instance, once a week there can be a certain time set a side for family activities, such as playing board games, athletic competitions, or a night on the town. Perhaps, these activities can be arranged so that the student gets to spend time solely with siblings or a particular parent. The student can select what he or she wants to do during this quality time, thus giving the student some control over the activity.

WHAT SKILLS ARE NEEDED TO IMPROVE SOCIAL BEHAVIOR?

Changing your students' environments and enhancing your teaching are a good beginning, but that's not all you need to do. In order to help your students, you'll have to teach them skills that will last a lifetime. There are several social skill curricula and resources on the market that can help you teach students with ADHD social skills. These include, but are not limited to:

- Adelman, H. S., and L. Taylor. "Enhancing the Motivation and Skills Needed to Overcome Interpersonal Problems." *Learning Disability Quarterly* 5 (1982): 438–45.
- Blackbourn, J. M. "Acquisition and Generalization of Social Skills in Elementary-Aged Children with Learning Disabilities." *Journal of Learning Disabilities* 22, (1989): 28–34.
- Camp, B. W., and M. A. Bash. *Think Aloud*. (Champaign, Ill.: Research Press, 1985).
- Center, D. B. *Curriculum and Teaching Strategies for Students with Behavioral Disorders*. (Englewood Cliffs, N.J.: Prentice Hall, 1989).
- Fister, S., and K. Kemp. *Social Skills Survival Kit*. (Longmont, Colo.: Sopris West, 1994).
- Goldstein, A. P., R. P. Sprafkin, N. J. Gershaw, and P. Klein. *Skillstreaming the Adolescent: A Structured Approach to Teaching Prosocial Skills*. (Champaign, Ill.: Research Press, 1980).
- Guevremont, D. "Social Skills and Peer Relationship Training." In *Attention-Deficit Hyperactivity Disorder,* ed. R. Barkley, 540–72. (New York: Guilford Press, 1990).
- Hamlett, K. W., D. S. Pelligrini, and C. K. Conners. "An Intervention of Executive Processes in the Problem-Solving of Attention

Deficit Disorder Hyperactive Children." *Journal of Pediatric Psychology* 12 (1987): 227–40.

- Higgins, P. *ASSIST Program.* (Longmont, Colo.: Sopris West, 1993).
- Hinshaw, S. P., B. N. Henker, and C. K. Whalen. "Self-Control in Hyperactive Boys in Anger-Inducing Situations: Comparative and Combined Effects." *Journal of Consulting and Clinical Psychology* 52 (1984): 739–49.
- Martin, J. E., and L. H. Marshall. "ChoiceMaker: A Comprehensive Self-Determination Transition Program." *Intervention in School and Clinic* 30, no. 3 (1995): 147–56.
- Schultze, K. A., S. Rule, and M. S. Innocenti. "Coincidental Teaching: Parents Promoting Social Skills at Home." *Teaching Exceptional Children* 21, no. 2 (1989): 24–27.
- Schumaker, J. B., J. S. Hazel, and C. S. Pederson. *Social Skills for Daily Living.* (Circle Pines, Minn.: American Guidance Service, 1988).
- Stephens, T. M. *From Social Skills in the Classroom.* (Columbus, Oh.: Cedar Press, 1978).
- Walker, H. M. *The Walker Social Skills Curriculum: The ACCEPTS Program.* (Austin, Tex.: PRO-ED, 1988).
- Walker, H. M., G. Colvin, and E. Ramsey. *Antisocial Behavior in Schools: Strategies and Best Practices.* (Pacific Grove, Calif.: Brooks/Cole, 1995).

In addition to entire curricula, there are several simple strategies you could use to teach your students valuable social skills. For example, you need to teach them how to make and maintain friendships, how to control their temper, and how to solve problems in a relationship. These strategies can be used at home, at school, and in the community.

Remembering Names

Have you ever been at a get-together and somebody introduces himself but as soon as he says his name, you have already forgotten it? Or how about if your date called you by the wrong name? Would you go out with that person again?

Remembering somebody's name is the first step in developing a friendship. Unfortunately, for individuals who are hyperactive or inattentive, remembering people's names can be difficult. If they can be taught strategies to remember people's names, they will be more likely to develop positive friendships.

One way that people remember names is to associate them with some characteristic of the person. For example, if somebody named Rudy has red hair, you can remember his name by pairing "Rudy" with "Red." Or if somebody named Al is tall, you can remember "Al" because it is part of "t - Al - l." Try using this strategy with your name.

Repeating somebody's name after they have said it is another way of remembering people's names. For example, when somebody says, "My name is Susie," you can reply, "It is very nice to meet you, Susie." You can also repeat her name to yourself until it sinks in.

Thinking before Speaking

Another skill that you should teach your students is to think before they speak. For individuals who are impulsive or hyperactive, monitoring what they are about to say is easier said than done. However, with practice, it is possible for students to develop this ability.

When a student approaches you, you might cue him to think about what he wants to say. You should also ask him to think about whether what he intends to say is appropriate for the given situation. This is a particularly effective strategy to use when a student is initiating a conversation with a peer.

Asking People Questions

Have you ever met somebody who only talked about himself or herself? Did you want to talk with that person again? Unfortunately, people who are socially immature tend to monopolize conversations. You will have to find ways to teach students to ask people questions.

There are several methods of teaching students to ask questions. For example, you can role-play interactions and help students identify appropriate questions that would keep the conversation going. You could also have students watch videotapes of conversations and have them brainstorm questions that they would have asked had they been one of the characters on tape.

Summarizing Conversations

Students who are inattentive often lose track of what other people are saying, thus making conversations one-sided. A strategy for helping students to keep focused during conversations is to mentally repeat the other person's main points. This will help students filter out extraneous information.

Being Aware of Other People's Nonverbal Language

Students with ADHD are often unaware of other people's emotions. For example, they keep talking even though their audience is giving clear indications that they are bored, such as looking at their watches or yawning. Being able to correctly interpret these signs is very important for successful communication.

One way of teaching students about nonverbal language is to use role-playing or tapes of people interacting. You can also have your students watch other students during lunch or during recess. Perhaps you could even have your students go to the mall after school and watch people shop. Have them observe the faces and body language of people who look at the price of an expensive outfit.

Being Aware of Your Nonverbal Language

Once students begin to understand nonverbal body language, have them examine their own body language. Again, you could use videotape for this strategy, or you can periodically have students "freeze" in place and ask them to examine how they are standing or where their arms are. You could then have them determine how other people might interpret their body language.

APPLYING WHAT YOU HAVE LEARNED

Have you ever seen the movie *Harvey*? It is about a lovable drunk, played by Jimmy Stewart, whose best friend is a 7'-2" invisible rabbit named Harvey. Throughout the movie, everybody is trying to convince Jimmy Stewart's character that he needs to "smarten up" and realize that Harvey does not exist. Jimmy Stewart replies, "You know, I was once told that in order to be successful in this world you have to be either really smart or really pleasant. Well, I was smart for a long time, and personally, I recommend being pleasant."

These are very poignant words and they apply to your students. Given a choice, would you rather help your students become very smart but socially maladjusted, or socially competent but intellectually simple? Think about that. Which is more important? Intelligence or social skills?

One could argue that, regardless of how intelligent you are, you couldn't lead a fruitful life without appropriate social skills. For example, your intelligence might help you professionally—you might cure cancer, make a billion dollars, and have all kinds of wonderful possessions—but without friends and loved ones with whom to share such things, life is empty. As the Beatles said, "Money can't buy me love."

Obviously, there has to be some sort of balance between academic and social intelligence. Where that balance lies is up to you and the rest of the IEP team to determine, but please note that much of what you will be teaching to children with ADHD will not be academic knowledge per se, but social skills.

Take, for instance, the case study about Raymond. Apparently, Raymond is doing well enough academically, but socially he is a mess. Can you image what his life is going to be like if he doesn't learn how to interact with women appropriately? He'll be a social outcast. He'll have very few friends, certainly few female friends, and, if he keeps touching women's breasts, he'll probably get arrested for sexual assault. To Raymond, developing social skills is far more important than learning academic tasks.

What do you think is behind Raymond's behaviors? Does he have ADHD? Or is there something else causing him to act inappropriately? How could you modify the environment so that he can learn to be more socially appropriate? What strategies would you use to teach him social skills? Finally, what skills would you teach him?

Does Raymond Have ADHD?

What do you think about Raymond? Does he have ADHD? If so, what type?

Let's look at the facts. Raymond's teacher indicated that Raymond is "inattentive" and "overactive." Further, his social skills seem to stem from impulsivity. That is, he simply does whatever pops into his mind. Moreover, these symptoms appear to adversely affect his life. If these symptoms have been present since childhood, Raymond could be diagnosed with ADHD-C. However, you certainly would need more conclusive evidence for an actual diagnosis.

What Other Conditions Could Explain Raymond's Behavior?

Let's suppose that Raymond doesn't have ADHD-C. What else could be causing his behavior? There are several possibilities.

First of all, Raymond could be drinking or taking drugs. Intoxicated individuals often have difficulty controlling their impulses, much like Raymond. Further, people under the influence might say things that they otherwise might not when sober. Distractibility and overactivity might also be caused by stimulants, such as cocaine. If Raymond's behavior is new, drug or alcohol use is likely to be an explanation.

Raymond's behavior also can be explained by various psychotic disorders, such as schizophrenia or schizoaffective disorder. Both of these conditions are characterized by delusions, which could prompt Raymond to behave inappropriately. For example, Raymond could hear voices telling him to touch women's breasts, or he could believe that all women are in love with him. Such disorders typically develop during, or shortly after, puberty, which seems to fit Raymond's case.

A more likely non-ADHD explanation for Raymond's behavior is that he simply is a socially immature teenage male. Think about teenagers that you know. Think about yourself when you were their age. Did you act "odd," as Raymond's teacher put it? Sometimes, teenagers just don't know how to act around the opposite sex. As a result, they do goofy things.

How Would You Change Raymond's Environments?

Regardless of why Raymond is acting socially inappropriate, you have to do something. No matter the cause, touching somebody's body without permission cannot be tolerated. Altering the environment might help prevent some of the problems.

You might want to remove the temptation for Raymond to say and do things without thinking. You could do this in several ways. For example, you can have him sit away from his friends who encourage him to misbehave. You also could have Raymond sit near your more responsible male students.

These strategies will do three things. First, with Raymond's friends away from him, he might be less likely to act inappropriately. Second, with male students sitting around him, he won't be able to touch female students, at least not while sitting in his seat. Finally, the male students can model appropriate behavior.

What Strategies Would You Use to Teach Raymond?

How would you teach Raymond social skills? You could lecture him or show him videos. Perhaps you could role-play various situations, or use workbooks or specially designed curricula. Each of these might do the trick, but you might consider something else.

Sometimes the best teacher is not the adult standing in front of the class, but the students who are staring at the chalkboard. If you want Raymond to develop social skills, he'll have to gain a sense of what is appropriate and what is inappropriate behavior.

One way of doing this is to have Raymond meet with a group of older female students, perhaps high school students. Have these students meet with Raymond once a week to discuss how women want to be treated. For example, they can help Raymond understand how to approach a woman without saying insulting things or touching her body.

Further, this strategy could be used as part of a reward system. For instance, if Raymond goes the entire week without being socially inappropriate, he is allowed to meet with the female students. In essence, the strategy teaches and reinforces itself.

What Skills Would You Teach Raymond?

In addition to math, English, and all of the other academic subjects, you will need to teach some students social skills. For example, you might have to teach them how to initiate and maintain a conversation, or how to participate in a conversation without dominating it. In the case of Raymond, what skills would you teach him?

One skill that he desperately needs is self-monitoring. Raymond should think about what he wants to say before he actually says it. He also needs to understand other people's feelings. Perhaps if he understands other peoples' perspectives, he will refrain from making comments like, "You could stand to lose ten pounds."

CHAPTER 6

Strategies for Children with ADHD

CHAPTER OBJECTIVES

This chapter answers the following questions:

1. What is ADHD like during childhood?
2. How can you help families?
3. How can you teach children with ADHD?

CASE STUDY: BOBBY

Bobby is a five-year-old student who has been kicked out of our pre-school program. It isn't a decision that we are happy about. It is just that he never sat still, refused to follow directions, broke things on purpose, frequently talked back to our staff, and had a tendency of becoming physically aggressive with peers and adults.

We met with Bobby's parents on several occasions, but they did not help the situation. Bobby's father is a very successful doctor and feels that Bobby is a good kid, but needs to be challenged academically. He claims that we are not stimulating his son enough and that is why Bobby is acting out.

Bobby's mother is a stay-at-home mom. She is very frustrated and doesn't know what to do with her son. She reports that she tries to discipline Bobby, but he just doesn't listen to her. He simply laughs and runs away whenever she yells at or spanks him.

Bobby's older sister came to our last meeting. She indicated that Bobby frequently messes with her stuff and constantly wants to be around her. She hates always having to baby-sit him and feels that he is preventing her from going out with her friends.

At our last staff meeting, we referred Bobby to be tested for ADHD. His parents, however, declined. As a result, Bobby is no longer attending our classes.

Case Study Questions

1. Do you think Bobby has ADHD? Explain.
2. What else could be causing Bobby's behavior?
3. How would you help Bobby's family?
4. What strategies would you use to teach Bobby?

WHAT IS ADHD LIKE DURING CHILDHOOD?

Think back for a moment to when you were in elementary school or preschool, or picture children that you have seen at the mall, playground, or various fast food restaurants. Can you picture them running around, getting so excited about everything? Maybe they are displaying mood swings—one minute they are very happy, then they are crying, then they are happy again. They probably even are demanding something with great vigor, but when they get it, it is as if they have forgotten why they want it. These behaviors are typical of children.

Now image that those children have ADHD! They are probably running around twice as much, climbing all over things, and asking tons of questions (or the same questions over and over again) but never staying around to hear the answers. They are probably bullying the other kids or playing by themselves. Now imagine that you are the parent of an ADHD child. Feeling a little overwhelmed?

In many ways, working with children who have ADHD is the same as working with adolescents or adults with ADHD. Children, adolescents, and adults with ADHD all may exhibit periods of inattentiveness, hyperactivity, impulsivity, and poor social skills. However, children with ADHD have several issues different from those faced by older students with ADHD.

For example, suppose you had two classrooms. One was at the twelfth-grade level, the other at the first-grade level. In both classrooms, you have students with ADHD. Both groups have difficulties maintaining their attention late in the day. However, despite their similarities, you probably would use different strategies for each of these classes.

With the older students, you might use a metacognition strategy, such as having the students record on a chart how often they were on task. You might also teach the older students how to take notes and keep a "to do" list to remind them when assignments are due. Would you use these strategies for your younger students?

Probably not. First graders—still working on their colors, numbers, and letters—might not understand the concept of metacognition. Further, because a typical first grader is just learning how to write, having your younger students with ADHD take notes and keep lists is impractical.

In addition to developmental level, studies have found significant differences between parents of young children with ADHD and parents of older ADHD students. Specifically, mothers of preschoolers with ADHD initially report that they are able to manage their children's behaviors. However, by the time their children enter elementary school, parents indicate that they are unable to control their children. Further, the capability of parents to deal with inappropriate behavior decreases as their children get older (Mash and Johnston 1983).

Studies have also found that parents of children with ADHD are far more likely to suffer from depression, low self-esteem, and be socially isolated than parents of non-ADHD children (Befera and Barkley 1985; Cunningham, Benness, and Siegel 1988; Mash and Johnston 1983). These symptoms, as well as the severity of the maladaptive behavior, increase as children with ADHD grow older. This could explain why children who have ADHD are more likely to be physically abused by family members than children without ADHD (Heffron, Martin, Welsh, and Perry 1987).

Further, parents of children with ADHD interact with their children differently than do other parents. For instance, mothers of children with ADHD tend to give more commands and directions than other parents. Parents of children with ADHD also criticize and punish their children more than other parents (Barkley 1988; Campbell 1990).

Finally, family members of children with ADHD (e.g., parents, brothers, and sisters) experience more stress than individuals in other families. Consequently, there tend to be higher rates of drug and alcohol abuse, domestic violence, and suicide in families of children with ADHD. Parents of children with ADHD are also more likely to divorce than parents of children without ADHD (Barkley 1995).

If you teach at the preschool or elementary school level, or if you have young children with ADHD, you have a lot to think about. Not only do you have to modify strategies so that they can be applied to young students, but you must also work with family members to reduce their stress. Working with the families is crucial. Imagine how you would act at school if you were getting abused at home, if your family members were always yelling at you, or if your parents were getting a divorce. Education is more than worksheets, seating charts, and discipline. You have to communicate effectively with parents nearly everyday. You also have to teach family members about their child's disability. Further, you have to show them how they too can teach their child. In essence, both you and your students should expect a lot of "home" work.

HOW CAN YOU HELP FAMILIES?

In order to help your students, you must help their families. You will need to teach family members about ADHD and what strategies they can use to minimize problem behaviors at home. You'll also have to give them emotional support and resources for future use. Here are several ways to do this.

Parent and Sibling Training

One very important way to help families is to educate parents, siblings, and other family members of children about ADHD. It is important to educate the entire family; by training just one parent, you could increase family stress by making that parent the only caregiver of the child with ADHD.

To educate families, you could put on workshops for family members of children with ADHD once or twice a semester. Topics could include: What is ADHD? When should medication be used? How should I teach and discipline my child? What are some ways to reduce stress at home? There are several resources in the literature that might be able to help you develop a family training program. In addition to the other texts listed in chapter 10 they include, but are not limited to:

- Blechman, E. A. *Solving Child Behavior Problems at Home and at School.* (Champaign, Ill.: Research Press, 1985).
- Clark, L. *SOS: Help for Parents: A Practical Guide for Handling Common Everyday Behavior Problems.* Bowling Green, Ky.: Parents Press, 1985).

- Dubey, D. R., S. G. O'Leary, and K. F. Kaufman. "Training Parents of Hyperactive Children in Child Management: A Comparative Outcome Study." *Journal of Abnormal Child Psychology* 11, (1983): 229–46.
- Erhardt, D., and B. L. Baker. "The Effects of Behavioral Parent Training on Families with Young Hyperactive Children." *Journal of Behavior and Experimental Psychiatry* 21, no. 2 (1990): 121–32.
- Strayhorn, J. M., and C. S. Weidman. "Reduction of Attention Deficit and Internalizing Symptoms in Preschoolers through Parent-Child Interaction Training." *Journal of the American Academy of Child and Adolescent Psychiatry* 28, no. 6 (1989): 888–96.
- Strayhorn, J. M., and C. S. Weidman. "Follow-up One Year after Parent-Child Interaction Training: Effects on Behavior of Preschool Children." *Journal of the American Academy of Child and Adolescent Psychiatry* 30, no. 1 (1991): 138–43.

Respite Care

Respite care is simply another way of saying "giving family members a chance to get away from the stress at home and relax." Imagine that you had to spend all day, everyday, with one of your family members. Even though you probably love that person very much, overexposure to anybody probably would drive you crazy. Now image that that person was a child with ADHD. You would probably need a lot of time to yourself.

There are many forms of respite care. Parents could simply hire a baby-sitter each Friday night so that the rest of the family can experience life without an ADHD child, or families can have an extended family network where children spend an occasional weekend or summer vacation with grandparents or cousins. However, please do not forget the needs of the respite care providers. They will need training as well, especially older grandparents who don't have the energy to keep up with a hyperactive preschooler. Invite them to your workshops, create a pool of trained baby-sitters, and give parents resources (e.g., a "tip sheet") that they can forward to extended family members.

Families need to spend time together *and* away from each other. Many parents feel guilty and refuse to admit that they want to spend time away from their child. You have to assure them that the need for individual time is crucial for everybody, regardless of having a child with ADHD. Further, all parents need time to be a couple, if only to strengthen their marital relationship.

Respite for Siblings

Do you have a sibling? Did you have to take care of that sibling when you were younger? Did the sibling have to take care of you? All older siblings are forced to take the role of a caregiver from time to time. If taking care of children with ADHD is hard for you as a teacher or parent, think how hard it is for another child.

Older siblings should help in any way they can. However, parents need to know their older children's limits. They must also give their older children opportunities to be themselves, away from their brothers or sisters with ADHD. Siblings need support, training, and stress reduction—just as their parents and you do.

Support Groups

What do you do when you have parents who desperately need a break from their child, but refuse to admit it? You could try to reason with them, but that might not work. An effective way of helping parents who are in denial is to introduce them to other parents of children with ADHD. This could be done through support groups.

Support groups can be of tremendous help in many ways. For example, parents can share information on ADHD, resources in the community (e.g., who the best doctors and therapists are), and what methods seem to work best when teaching their children. Further, support groups allow parents to feel as if they are not alone. Support groups also give parents assurances that they did not cause their child's ADHD and that they are not bad parents. There are also support groups for siblings of children with ADHD. (Please see chapter 10 for lists of support groups and other resources.)

Communication between Parents and Teachers

One of the many stressors that parents and teachers of children with ADHD experience is the teacher-parent relationship. Teachers often come off as "the professionals" and that they "know best." Further, teachers are often treated by parents as "obstacles" or as "adversaries."

This is particularly true of parents who know their rights and have a strong desire to be involved in their child's education. Effective communication is the key to building collaborative relationships and preventing misunderstandings.

As a special educator, one way that you can build effective communication with the parents or teachers is to increase your contact with them. Make a ritual of sending notes home or to school. Call parents or teachers just to say hello. Have monthly meetings or get-togethers. Keep a journal on how the student is doing and send it back and forth between school and home. You could even use e-mail to communicate on a regular basis. In other words, by the time you have your first IEP meeting, parents and teachers should already know each other and be on the way to developing a mutual respect.

Another way of cultivating this respect is to show parents that you care about them and their children. Give them resources. Call them up when there is new information on ADHD. Allow them to facilitate the IEP meetings, or even socialize with them without bringing up ADHD or education.

Probably the most important component of building a successful relationship with parents and teachers is to be positive. Ever been around somebody who only had negative things to say? Well, for many parents, that is what it is like to be around teachers. They ask teachers how their child is doing and the teachers spew forth a list of all the awful things that their child has done.

Teachers, of course, shouldn't lie to the parents. On the contrary, effective relationships are also built on trust. Instead of giving all negative information, try to say a few good things about the child for every negative thing. For example, instead of saying, "Your child is constantly out of his seat," you could say something like, "Your child sure has a lot of energy. He is frequently jumping out of his seat to do something across the room. If we can just find a way to channel his energy, he will really go far in life." Remember, having ADHD is not a bad thing. It can be a gift if a child is able to use it. Remind parents of that frequently

Stress Reduction

Whether as a parent or as a teacher, one of the skills that you will need to master is how to reduce and prevent stress. Everybody is different.

COLLABORATING WITH
RELUCTANT PARENTS OR TEACHERS

Whatever role you play in the education of a child with ADHD, you will work with individuals who, for whatever reason, don't like you or don't like what you represent. For example, a parent might feel that you don't care about her child, or a regular education teacher might feel that you are trying to "push those kids" into his classroom. How you approach these occasions will determine how successful a teacher you will be. Below are some tips to keep in mind when collaborating with reluctant parents or teachers.

- Keep the other person's perspective in mind. If parents seem reluctant to work with you, remember that it is their child and they have a lot more to lose than you do.
- Identify the source of resistance and then address it. For example, many teachers do not want a student with ADHD in their class because they are worried that the student will require all of their time at the expense of their thirty other students. If this is the case, address the concern. Figure out ways of supporting the teachers. Team teach. Demonstrate strategies that effectively address behavior problems.
- Shut your mouth and genuinely listen to what others are saying.
- Provide feedback. Make sure there are no miscommunications.
- Realize that sometimes people have bad days and it has nothing to do with you.
- Remember that the key word is "collaboration" not "dictation." If parents and teachers are reluctant to work with you, perhaps it is because they believe you only want things your way. In order to be a successful teacher, sometimes you have to do what other people want. Don't forget, you work for the student and the parents. They don't work for you.
- Never verbally attack other people or their ideas. If you ever find yourself in a situation where you have been less than polite, apologize when things cool down. Sometimes, a lot can get done when people are making up after a fight.
- Not everything has to be settled right away. Sometimes it is okay to agree to disagree and move on to more pressing topics.
- Allow people to process information. Ideally, developing an IEP plan should not be done in one sitting. IEPs are far too important to be developed in a rushed manner.
- Have meetings on other people's "home turf." Meet with parents at their homes or a neutral place that they suggest, such

as a restaurant. Meet with regular educators in their class-room or office.
- The past is the past. Don't let past arguments creep into present conversations.
- There are no bad ideas, especially when you are brainstorming. Even the most apparently asinine suggestion might have merit—you just have to look for it.

You might like to sit in front of the television when you get stressed. Some of your friends might like to go dancing. Whatever the outlet, you will need to figure out what works best for you and the parents of your students. Here are some suggestions.

- *Joining a health club.* Exercise not only helps reduce stress, but it also helps prevent stress from returning. Further, joining a health club will give you opportunities to interact with other adults and make new friends.
- *Develop hobbies.* Have interests other than education and ADHD. Gardening, painting, writing are all great examples of stress-reducing hobbies.
- *Read for pleasure.* Reading is a great way to spend time by your-self and "decompress" after a hard day. Books on tape are also use-ful during the long drives to and from work.
- *Talk with somebody.* Tell your friends what is putting pressure on you. Therapists are great ways of releasing pent-up tension.
- *Go to a spa.* Nothing is quite as relaxing as a body massage or sit-ting in a hot tub. Splurge once in a while; go to a spa.
- *Time management.* Schedule your life effectively. Give yourself plenty of downtime or time just for yourself. Schedule weekly or monthly activities with friends, such as playing poker or going to the movies. Prioritize what you have to do, what you want to do, and what you should do. Do whatever you have to do to reward yourself. You deserve it!

Response Delay

Ever hear an adult counting to ten at a restaurant after his child spilled a drink all over? This is a very good strategy for dealing with upsetting situations. It is called "response delay." Basically, you try not to respond impulsively right after the child does something wrong.

Think about it. As soon as a child spills a drink, what is your first instinct? You would probably want to yell, right? That is only natural. Unfortunately, it is not exactly helpful. Ever hear of the expression, "No use crying over spilled milk?" All you are going to do is upset the kid and escalate the situation.

If you wait for a few seconds, you can suppress your natural desire to yell. Further, you will be able to reassess the situation and come up with a more positive approach. For example, you could say, "Accidents happen, but you'll have to clean it up yourself."

Seeing the Positive

All too often, parents and teachers see only the small, negative stuff. They don't see much of the positive things that children do. In the above example, it is really easy to look at spilling a drink as a negative situation. However, there are ways to see it as a positive one. For example, maybe the child said that she was sorry—something that she wouldn't have done a couple months earlier. Same with actually cleaning the mess up. Two months ago, the child might have refused. In other words, you can choose to look at something negatively, or you can choose to look at it positively. Sometimes finding the positive takes time, but it is always there.

Focusing on the War, Not the Battles

Parents and teachers also have a tendency of focusing on the battles, the day-to-day situations, that give them grief. They tend to fixate on the fact that the child was late getting ready for school or that she forgot her lunch. These are all very small potatoes and not worth losing sleep over.

Think about the long-term outcomes—the war. Think about how the child used to behave last year. Think of all of the skills that she has learned since then. Everybody is going to have good and bad days; so are your students. If you focus on the long term, there will undoubtedly be more good days than bad. Perhaps keeping a list of the good versus bad days would help illustrate this fact.

HOW CAN YOU TEACH CHILDREN WITH ADHD?

In addition to changing how you perceive certain events, you will need to begin modifying the child's behaviors at school and at home. Addressing behavioral issues early on is very important; the longer the child is allowed to act inappropriately, the harder it will be for the child to learn and fit in socially later on in life. Many of the strategies discussed earlier in this text will help you teach children with ADHD. However, preschoolers and students in elementary school have additional issues that may require additional interventions.

Picture Lists

One intervention that can be used with young children is to use picture lists. It is often difficult to work with young children because they require a great amount of attention. For example, children with ADHD frequently forget their assignments, supplies, or what they are supposed to be doing. With older students, you can make them keep a list of their assignments and activities; however, younger students might not know how to read or write. In these situations, you could compile lists using pictures of sight words. Such a strategy would make children with ADHD less reliant on your constant reminders, thus decreasing chances of creating dependence.

Time

Another skill that older students have that young children don't is telling time. Remember going on vacation with your parents when you were a kid? Every five minutes, you asked, "Are we there yet?" Each time, your parents probably told you that you would reach your destination in a couple of hours. Unfortunately, to young children who don't know how to tell time, the phrase "in a couple of hours" is meaningless, so you were forced to keep checking if you were almost where you wanted to be.

One thing that your parents could have done was to give you a kitchen timer. After the timer's bell went off the first time, you would be half the way to your destination. The second time, you would almost be there. You can use the same strategy for children with ADHD.

Any occasion that involves time needs to have an accommodation. For example, suppose that you or some parents are using a "time out" strategy. Every time a child acts out, they have to go sit in the corner for ten minutes. Unfortunately, people with ADHD tend to have a lousy sense of time. Children with ADHD are even worse. They are likely to sit in the time-out chair and think that the time is up after only a few minutes. When they get up to go back to their desk, they will get into even more trouble.

In addition to using timers, you could have the student match his object to another. For example, many preschool and early elementary classrooms have play clocks that allow you to move the minute and hour hands. When a child needs to do something at a certain time, such as leave time-out, set the play clock for that time. The student can then look at the real clock and wait for it to match the play clock.

Be Very Clear and Concise

As with all children, you need to be very clear and concise. This is especially true when children are being disciplined. Do you remember when you were a child and you did something wrong? Did your teacher or parents stand there yelling at you for several minutes as they wagged their finger up and down? Did you pay attention to them? At first you probably did, but after a few sentences your parents and teachers started to sound like cartoon characters saying, "blah, blah, blah, blah, blah, blah."

One of the primary characteristics of people with ADHD is difficulty *maintaining* attention. Even children without ADHD have difficulty paying attention to their parents and teachers. Don't flood students with needless information. Tell them exactly what you want them to do and that's it.

Ask Yes/No Questions

It is also important for you to ask very simple questions. Try to keep them to yes or no answers. If you turn and find that the pet bird is flying around the room, don't ask the child standing by the cage "How did the bird get out?" The last thing you want is a long drawn-out explanation that gives you no information. Instead ask, "Did you let the bird out?" It is clear, concise, and requires a straightforward answer; however, there is no guarantee that your student will fess-up to letting the bird out. Kids, after all, are kids.

ADHD AND THE PERCEPTION OF TIME

Without looking at a clock, try to estimate when it was that you last took a break from reading. Was it fifteen minutes ago? Twenty? An hour? Now look at your watch. How close were you to the actual time?

Have you ever sat through a really boring class and you could have sworn that it was almost over, but when you looked at the clock, you suddenly realized that you still had more than an hour left in the period? That is how students with ADHD feel most of the time. Students with ADHD have a very poor sense of time. To them, thirty minutes may feel like five minutes or an hour.

This difficulty estimating the passage of time causes many problems for students with ADHD. For instance, students with ADHD tend to believe they have more time than they actually do. This explains why they tend to turn in homework late, miss deadlines, and show up late for class or their curfew. They also have difficulty waiting or being patient because they feel as if they have been waiting much longer than they actually have.

There are several strategies that teachers and parents can use to help students with ADHD better manage their time. For example, you could get the student a watch with multiple alarms. Set the alarms for key times, such as thirty-minutes before their curfew starts or when they are supposed to be home for dinner. The alarm will serve as a reminder that they have to stop what they are doing and head home.

Another strategy is to break down assignments so that there are several recent deadlines rather than one deadline several days or weeks away. This could help the student focus on the task and prevent procrastination.

You can also give students a "month at a glance" calendar. Then have the students indicate on each date what is due. Further, have the students cross out each passing day so they are able to see how much time they have left before major projects are due.

There are several methods of circumventing issues caused by students' poor perception of time. Most can involve visual or auditory cues (e.g., alarm clocks). In order to help students internalize these strategies, however, they should be used consistently in multiple environments—especially at home. Additionally, students have to get into the habit of self-monitoring their usage of time so that they are able to succeed in environments without parents and teachers.

Give Only One Direction

Some older hyperactive students thrive when they have a number of activities that they can work on all at the same time. Preschoolers and elementary students tend not to have this ability. As a result, try giving children with ADHD only one direction at a time.

For example, say "Put your toys away." When they have done that, say "Now put your dirty clothes in the hamper." When they have done that, say "Get ready for dinner." And so on. This is much better than telling them everything all at once.

Once your students are able to follow single directions. Try to build their "endurance." You can start giving them two directions, such as "Get out your paper and pencil." Eventually, your students should be able to follow a string of commands without forgetting.

Getting Attention

When talking to a child with ADHD, make sure that you have their attention. Use the student's name. Make sure they are looking directly in your eyes before you begin speaking. Start by asking a simple "yes/no" question. This will help ascertain whether they are paying attention or merely staring through you. Then tell them very clearly and concisely what you want them to do.

Provide a Lot of Structure

Remember that younger students haven't been in school very long. They may not have gotten used to the notion of being in a structured environment. For instance, they probably are not in the habit of asking if it is okay to go to the bathroom. They just get up and leave the classroom. As a result, it is important to provide students with a lot of consistent structure. Providing a daily routine where students know what to expect will help.

Teach the Student about ADHD

More so than anything else, you must teach children what ADHD means. However, how you do this may have some disastrous effects. For example, suppose that a student is having a real hard time learning something, such as colors, the alphabet, or adding. What do you think the long-term consequences would be if you or the parents said, "Oh, it's okay if you can't do that; it's because you have ADHD." You have created a sense of "learned helplessness," the child's belief that he can't do things before he even tries.

How you teach children about ADHD could set the tone for the rest of their lives. You'll have to paint an honest picture of the condition but also be very positive. Remember, ADHD is not, in and of itself, a bad thing. People with ADHD have a lot of energy and can be very creative. However, make sure that you explain all of this in a way that your students can understand.

You might want to explain ADHD to children in this way. Talk to them about their favorite superhero. Bring up the fact that each superhero has different abilities. For example, Superman can fly and has super strength. Spiderman can climb up walls and shoot webs. And Wonderwoman can fly her invisible jet and make people tell the truth.

Then explain that people in real life are a lot like superheroes—everybody has different abilities. Some children can play kickball really well. Others can remember the entire alphabet and count to one hundred. Still others can tell jokes and make people laugh.

The super abilities of kids with ADHD include having a lot of energy and being able to run around a lot without getting tired. They can also be very creative and intelligent. The purpose of school and IEPs is to get children with ADHD to control and utilize their super abilities for "The Good." In other words, by teaching students useful skills, you are helping them learn how to become superheroes. Or stated another way, you are teaching Superman how to fly.

APPLYING WHAT YOU HAVE LEARNED

Children with ADHD present educators with two problems that older students with ADHD do not exhibit. First, like all children, they have difficulty reading, telling time, and often do not have fully developed attention spans. Second, family members of children with ADHD experience high levels of stress and depression. They often blame themselves for the poor behavior of their children.

Consider the case study of Bobby at the beginning of the chapter. What do you think? Does Bobby have ADHD? What type? What would you do if you were his preschool teacher? How would you help his family?

Does Bobby Have ADHD?

Bobby certainly seems like a handful. However, would you diagnose him with ADHD, or is he merely a typical rowdy, five-year-old boy? Perhaps Bobby simply needs to be challenged more, much like his father said. Which do you think is correct? Let's take a look at the facts.

First, Bobby is five years old, so his behaviors are present during the appropriate time period for ADHD. Second, Bobby has many characteristics of a child with ADHD-HI or ADHD-C. Specifically, he doesn't sit still, he walks around when he shouldn't, he obviously has a lot of energy, he has difficulty playing with others, and he is inattentive. Third, Bobby's behavior is evident in multiple environments, in the classroom and at home.

Although it would seem that Bobby meets the criteria for ADHD, you might not want to diagnose him right away. Remember, a misdiagnosis could haunt Bobby and his family for the rest of their lives. You need to be sure that you have an accurate picture of who Bobby is. As always, consider other possible explanations for Bobby's behavior prior to an official diagnosis.

What Else Could Cause Bobby's Behavior?

Diagnosing young children with ADHD is often very difficult. In the case of Bobby, it is almost impossible to determine whether Bobby's behavior is the result of ADHD or being an energetic five year old. So how could you decide which is the proper diagnosis?

In the case of Bobby, you might want to begin by assuming that his behavior is the result of being five years old. In essence, you are giving him the benefit of the doubt. Further, by deferring the diagnosis of ADHD until a later date, you will be able to gather more data, which should enable you to make a more accurate diagnosis. However, you need to do more than just observe Bobby. Bobby and his family obviously need help. There appears to be a great deal of tension and stress within their family.

How Could You Help Bobby's Family?

The problems that Bobby's family is experiencing are typical of most families with hyperactive children. For example, his mother is a prime candidate for depression. His father may be either in denial or is unaware of what Bobby is like when he is not around. Finally, Bobby's sister appears frustrated by her brother and socially isolated.

There are several ways that you could help Bobby's family. For example, you could suggest that the mother get a day to herself each week; perhaps she could have a night on the town with her daughter. This could help reduce stress for both of them. Further, if the father takes care of Bobby when the mother is gone, he may gain a better understanding of his son's behavior as well as give him an opportunity of challenging his son academically.

You might also encourage Bobby's parents to give their daughter her own personal space. Perhaps allow her to have a lock on her bedroom door or allow her to go out with her friends once for every day she baby sits her brother. Further, if the daughter is going to baby-sit, she should be taught effective behavior management techniques. In fact, the entire family could benefit from in-services on disciplining children. Apparently, from what is written in the case study, Bobby's mother is only yelling at her son and spanking him. Other strategies should be tried.

How Could You Teach Bobby?

If you were Bobby's teacher or parent, what would you do? What would you teach him? What strategies would you use?

Before developing interventions and teaching strategies, you might want to compare Bobby's behavior with those of his peers. Are there any significant differences? Either way, you might want to examine your expectations. Are you expecting too much from a five-year-old child who has never been in a structured environment before? Perhaps he will calm down in a couple weeks, once he gets into the swing of things.

If Bobby does have a problem with attention and behavior, you should attempt to gradually increase his capacity for being on task. Try rewarding his appropriate behavior with M&Ms or additional play time. Further, give Bobby only one direction at a time. When he is able to follow one direction, begin giving him two-step directions. Also, remind Bobby of the classroom rules frequently. Have him say them out loud at the beginning of the day and after lunch. Lastly, communicate with Bobby's family members and teachers regularly, making sure that you tell them positive things in addition to areas of concern.

CHAPTER 7

Strategies for Adolescents with ADHD

CHAPTER OBJECTIVES

This chapter answers the following questions:

1. What is ADHD like during adolescence?
2. How can you increase a student's self-esteem?
3. How can you help students gain independence and control?

CASE STUDY: PAUL

Paul is a fourteen-year-old male student who is currently repeating the seventh grade. Although he displays considerable artistic talents, especially in drawing, painting, and music, he exhibits little motivation to learn academic subjects. In fact, he rarely goes to any class that isn't directly related to his artistic interests. Further, when he attends these classes, he rarely pays attention—thus resulting in his present failing grades in math, science, English, history, and gym. When asked why he doesn't care about academic subjects, Paul replies that they will not help him become a musician. He sometimes adds, "I am not very good with my head anyway." If his grades don't improve, he will be held back for the second straight year.

Of late, Paul has become increasingly hostile toward his parents and teachers. On three occasions, neighbors have called the police because they thought that Paul was going to hurt his family. Though his parents denied that they were in any danger, Paul is capable of screaming a string of profanities that unnerved even the police officers who arrived at their home.

During a family therapy session, Paul admitted to "experimenting" with marijuana and alcohol, but denies that he uses them regularly.

Circumstantial evidence, such as half-empty paint cans in his room and the smell of paint on his clothes, suggests that he also gets high off of paint fumes. Paul denies that he "huffs."

If the present situation does not improve, Paul's future appears bleak. As it now stands, Paul plans on dropping out of school in two years and driving to Los Angeles to become a "rock 'n' roll" star. The relationship between Paul and his parents is becoming increasingly strained. It is likely that they will become estranged if a line of communication isn't built between everybody involved.

Case Study Questions

1. Do you think Paul has ADHD? Explain.
2. What other conditions could explain Paul's behavior?
3. How can you help improve Paul's self-esteem?
4. How can you help Paul gain independence and control over his life?

WHAT IS ADHD LIKE DURING ADOLESCENCE?

Adolescence. The word strikes fear in the hearts of parents and teachers alike. It is a time of change and turmoil as well as a time of emotions and uncertainty. Regardless of functioning level or disability, adolescence can be a difficult time for everybody involved.

Do you remember going through adolescence? Your body was changing; you began to experience intense emotions—such as a desire to be independent and resisting the notion of conformity. You probably felt that your parents and teachers were treating you like a child even though you considered yourself a grown-up. Fitting in probably surpassed the need to study. Perhaps you began to be sexually active or experimented with drugs and alcohol.

Adolescence can be a very difficult time for students with ADHD—as well as their families and teachers. Consider for a moment when you first became interested in dating. It was probably very awkward for you to express your emotions and to risk rejection from your peers. You might even have had problems understanding the "rules" of dating or how to determine when somebody else liked you.

Now imagine that you are impulsive, hyperactive, or have problems paying attention. Not only do you have difficulty with the subtle nuances of social interactions, but you have a tendency to say exactly what is on your mind as well. Do you think adolescence would be any easier?

Did you have any power struggles with your parents during adolescence? What were they like? Was there a lot of arguing? A lot of tension? Could you understand why your parents said no to you whenever you asked to stay out late or wanted to take the car or go to some party with your friends? Do you remember that near constant stress?

Now picture that you have more mood swings than most teenagers and that you tend to be overly aggressive. Imagine that you have a very low tolerance for frustration and you have difficulty controlling your impulses. You act first and think about the consequences later. Do you think your relationship with your parents would be a healthy one?

Adolescence can be a very troublesome time for many teenagers. For students with ADHD, however, this time is particularly grating. For example, students with ADHD frequently have problems with lying, stealing, truancy, and aggression (Barkley 1990). They also have a tendency to execute poor judgment and exhibit inappropriate social behaviors (Robin 1990). Further, adolescents with ADHD are more likely to smoke cigarettes, take drugs, abuse alcohol, and get into automobile accidents than their peers without ADHD (Barkley 1990; Bender 1997;

DETECTING DRUG AND ALCOHOL USE

The use of drugs and alcohol is a problem for students with and without ADHD. Unfortunately, studies have found that individuals with ADHD are far more likely to be drug abusers and alcoholics than peers without ADHD (Barkley 1990; McGee, Partridge, Williams, and Silva 1991). The question for you is, "How do you tell if one of your students is using drugs or alcohol?"

If you suspect that your students are using drugs and alcohol, review the warning signs listed below. DSM-IV contains detailed criteria for the identification of substance intoxication, abuse, dependence, and withdrawal. Consult the DSM-IV manual directly for more information.

Alcohol Intoxication

1. slurred speech
2. uncoordination
3. unsteady gait
4. rapid, involuntary oscillation of the eyes
5. impairment in memory or attention
6. profound lethargy and mental apathy

Cannabis Intoxication (Marijuana)

1. conjunctival injection
2. increased appetite
3. dry mouth
4. rapid heart rate

Cocaine Intoxication

1. confusion
2. rapid heart rate
3. psychomotor agitation or retardation
4. nausea or vomiting
5. pupillary dilation
6. apparent weight loss
7. elevated or retarded blood pressure
8. muscular weakness, shallow breathing, chest pain, or cardiac arrhythmias
9. chills or sweating

Inhalant Intoxication

1. dizziness
2. rapid, involuntary oscillation of the eyes
3. slurred speech
4. unsteady gait
5. uncoordination
6. lack of energy
7. delayed reflexes
8. psychomotor retardation
9. tremor
10. general muscle weakness
11. blurred or double vision
12. profound lethargy and mental apathy
13. euphoria

If you suspect that one of your students is using illegal substances, you should report it to the appropriate school official right away. Further, many states *require* teachers to file suspicion reports if they believe a student is using alcohol or drugs. If you are a teacher, find out what the appropriate procedures are for reporting suspected drug and alcohol use in your school.

Weiss and Hechtmann 1986). In fact, adolescents with ADHD are more than twice as likely to be arrested, three times more likely to fail a grade or be suspended, and eight times more likely to be expelled or drop out of school than their peers (Barkley 1990; Zentall 1993).

The seriousness of the situations in which most adolescents with ADHD find themselves cannot be understated. They are at a cross-roads. They can go forward and be successful in life or they can get lost and fall through the cracks of our educational system. You are the crossing guard assigned to that crossroads. It is up to you to help these students find their way.

Do not take the job lightly. It will be tiresome for you, the students, and their parents. There will be times when you will want to quit and that you feel that your students don't appreciate your efforts. When these times occur, remember that you too were an adolescent once and, with a little help, you made it though all right. So can your students.

HOW CAN YOU INCREASE A STUDENT'S SELF-ESTEEM?

One of the primary problems that students with ADHD face during their adolescent years involves self-esteem. Low self-esteem can manifest itself in many forms—drug and alcohol use, gang activity, depression, suicide, social isolation, poor grades, and many other trouble signs. But how do you determine whether a student has poor self-esteem? There are several instruments that can help you measure a student's self-concept, including:

- Coopersmith Self-Esteem Inventories (Coopersmith 1981)
- Culture-Free Self-Esteem Inventories (Battle 1992)
- Multidimensional Self-Concept Scale (Bracken 1992)
- Piers-Harris Children's Self-Concept Scale (Piers and Harris 1984)
- Self-Esteem Index (Brown and Alexander 1991)
- Student Self-Concept Scale (Gresham, Elliott, and Evans-Fernandez 1992)
- Tennessee Self-Concept Scale (Fitts and Roid 1988)

Once you have determined that your student has a poor self-concept, what do you do? First, you need to determine why the student feels worthless. Second, you need to remove the factors that are causing this feeling, or at least lessen their impact. Finally, you should empower the student to feel better about her or himself.

Identifying the Causes of Low Self-Esteem

Trying to find out why somebody has low self-esteem sounds easier than it is. It often takes skilled therapists years to determine why somebody suffers from a poor self-image. However, there are several ways that you might be able to get an insight into what your students are thinking and feeling.

The first way, of course, is to talk with them—really talk with them. Not just talk with them as a teacher or parent to a student, but person to person. Ask them questions and be genuinely interested in their answers. In order for you to get your students to share with you, you may have to share with them. Perhaps you could tell them some of the issues you faced as a teenager, but don't pretend to know what they are feeling. Listen and respond without being judgmental or prescriptive. Allow the student to be honest, even if that means you don't like what he or she is saying.

Another method of trying to determine the cause of your students' low self-esteem is to listen when they are talking to their peers. Perhaps eavesdropping is a bit underhanded, but you can learn a lot if you keep your ears open when you are walking down the hallways. Try to figure out what your students' main topics of conversations are. Are they complaining about their parents? Their siblings? Poor grades? Girls or boys? Determine what your students are talking about in the hallways and you are likely to find what they are thinking about during class.

You might also be able to determine the nature of your students' poor self-concept by examining their homework. For example, what are the topics of their stories for English class? Who are the main characters? How do the stories end? When you have students do book reports, what books do your students select? Do they have a common theme? This is not to say that a student who reads only Stephen King has some deepseated psychological problems, but it does give you something to talk about, especially if you like Stephen King too.

Positive Thinking

Have you ever felt badly about yourself after watching a depressing movie? Perhaps you empathized with the victim in the movie and that brought your mood down. Have you ever felt really inspired after watching a good movie? After "Rocky" was released, millions of people joined health clubs, started drinking raw eggs, and ran up stairs with their arms waving in the air. Are there songs that make you smile? Do any make you cry?

People's emotions are affected by many variables. Students with low self-esteem have to learn to monitor and control those variables so that the variables don't control them. There are many ways of doing this. For example, students can learn to monitor their thoughts. This is particularly important for students who are hyperactive or depressive.

Students who are hyperactive not only have a lot of physical energy, but they have a lot of mental energy as well. Have you ever heard people with ADHD talk about how their minds work? They often describe it as watching a wall of televisions, each of which is on a different channel. Sometimes, one or two of those televisions are showing "negative" programs. For example, a negative program could be a recurring vision of failing a test or being turned down for a date. These negative programs can take their toll on the student's self-esteem. Further, students are frequently not aware of these negative programs; they just feel depressed. Getting your students to monitor their many thoughts will help determine what is bothering them.

Once students determine what negative thoughts are bothering them, you need to help them replace those thoughts with more positive ones. One way is to expose the student to more positive variables. For example, have them watch their favorite "feel good" movie or listen to uplifting music; sometimes, simply smiling works just as well. Your students can also drive bad thoughts out of their mind by thinking good things, such as repeating "I am going to do well on the test. I am going to do well on the test." Meditation and mantras can be particularly useful when replacing negative thoughts.

Creative Visualization

Another way for students to change their negative thought patterns is to use creative visualization. Simply put, creative visualization is "guided daydreaming." For example, if a student is depressed because he is afraid to ask somebody out on a date, he can imagine the person saying "yes" when he asks her out; if a student has text anxiety, she could imagine sitting down at her desk, taking the test, and getting all of the questions correct. It takes some repetition to have the good feelings from the visualization to sink in, but the strategy can be very effective.

Opportunities for Success and Finding Self-Worth

In addition to making friends, students can build their self-esteem by experiencing success. Parents and teachers can provide students with opportunities for being successful. For example, ask questions that you know your students can answer correctly. This can build their confidence and encourage them to participate more often in discussions.

Also, breaking complex tasks into more manageable sections could help increase self-worth. For example, if your students have to write a lengthy research paper, they might feel overwhelmed by the enormity of the task and refuse to try. If you break the paper into steps, they are more likely to see the activity as something that they can and want to do. Steps to writing the paper could include: 1) having the student find an interesting topic, 2) having the student determine want she wants to know about the topic, and 3) finding the answers to her questions.

Breaking intimidating tasks down into smaller, more manageable steps is a strategy that students can use throughout their lives. For example, applying to colleges or jobs is often very overwhelming. You have to figure out what you want to major in, what schools have that major, what area of the country you like best, how expensive of a school you could afford, and what schools would accept your SAT or ACT scores. You then have to figure out how to get the applications for each school and financial aid department, and for living in the residence halls. If you always look at the big picture, you might be tempted to quit before you start; if you make a list of each task you have to do and check off each task after you do it, the big picture comes more into focus.

Experiencing Responsibility

Being trusted to take care of pets or classroom mascots can have a significant impact on your students' self-esteem. It shows them that you have faith in their abilities. It also gives students a sense of purpose. In addition to animals, students could take care of a garden or a neighborhood park. Local volunteer programs, such as Habitat for Humanity, the Humane Society, and homeless shelters also offer students an opportunity to increase their self-esteem by experiencing responsibility and helping the community.

Self-Reflection

Often, when things get really bad in somebody's life, it is easy to forget the good times. This is particularly true for people who suffer from depression. When people are in a depressed mood, they are unable to remember the last time they smiled or were happy. Keeping a journal or a diary can help. When students begin to feel down, they can read passages in their journals and remember that things weren't always bad. Further, they can read about the bad times and how things always got better.

Support Groups

Frequently, people think support groups are just for adults. The truth is, there are many support groups for a variety of situations. For example, there are support groups for children of alcoholics, children of divorced parents, children who are adopted, and children who are biracial. There are also support groups for individuals with attention disorders. Information regarding these and other helpful support groups can be found in chapter 10.

HOW CAN YOU HELP STUDENTS
GAIN INDEPENDENCE AND CONTROL?

Adolescence is the period between childhood and adulthood. In addition to issues with self-esteem, adolescence is also characterized by a desire to gain independence and control over one's life. Unfortunately, if students are to gain control, somebody else must be willing to lose control. For teachers and parents, relinquishing power can be a frightening thing and often produces power struggles with teenagers. To optimize the learning potential of this period, strategies must be implemented that not only allow students to govern aspects of their life but also teach them how to make choices and behave responsibly.

Allow Students to Make Choices

Making choices is the very foundation of independence. However, making good choices and appropriate goals is a learned activity. It takes practice and guidance. There are several ways to give students the practice they need.

For example, give students options when doing assignments. Perhaps they can choose the book on which they do a book report, or maybe they can select whether they do an oral presentation or a written paper. In fact, the entire curriculum could be based on giving choices.

Students should also be given options at home. For instance, they might elect to clean the garage once a month rather than taking the trash out twice a week, or they can decide what is for dinner every Wednesday. Choices can be made everywhere.

There are even computer games that teach students to make choices and face the consequences. Have you ever heard of SimCity or SimIsland? With these computer games, the students have to make decisions to obtain a certain goal. For example, with SimIsland, the students have to turn a tropical island into a thriving civilization without destroying the island's beauty and natural resources. Each decision has repercussions that affect the progress to the ultimate goal. There are even games simulating home economics where students must budget their money and time in order to raise a family.

Giving students choices should be done at every age, but especially during adolescence. Making choices can build the students' self-esteem and sense of identity. Further, by learning from their mistakes, students can experience life's best teacher.

Student-Run IEPs

One of the best ways of giving students control over their lives is letting them run their own IEP meetings. Teach your students what has to be included in individualized educational plans and then let them run the entire production. Have them invite whomever they want to the meeting, have them summarize all of the reports, have them develop their own goals and objectives, and finally, have the students type the document and monitor its implementation. Not only is this strategy in compliance with the philosophy driving IDEA (Individuals with Disabilities Education Act), but it also gives students an opportunity to become vested in their education and future.

Independent Learning

Another strategy for enabling your students to become autonomous is to have them learn independently. To do this, you can give your students guidelines for what they need to learn but it is up to them to determine how they learn the material and demonstrate their knowledge. For example, suppose that you are teaching a unit on the conversion of water molecules to a gaseous state. Explain to your students that they must somehow demonstrate to you that they understand how water becomes a gas as well as why this process is important to humans. They can learn the information any way they wish, such as from the books on reserve in the school's library, videos from the Discovery Channel, or going to the Museum of Science and Industry. However, by the end of the week, they will have to demonstrate their knowledge, such as through a written report, an oral quiz, a diagram, or scientific experiment.

APPLYING WHAT YOU HAVE LEARNED

Adolescence is a time of change. It is the bridge that connects childhood to adulthood. Unfortunately, for teenagers with ADHD, adolescence can be the beginning of a road to social isolation, academic failure, and problems with the drugs, alcohol, and the law. If your students are to become successful adults, they will need to have self-worth and positive relationships.

Consider for a moment the case study at the beginning of this chapter. Do you think that Paul has ADHD? What other conditions could explain his behavior? As a parent or as a teacher, how could you help Paul build his self-esteem? How could you help him gain some independence and control over his life?

Does Paul Have ADHD?

Paul definitely has issues similar to those of adolescents with ADHD. He has problems managing his emotion. He has difficulty expressing himself. He is experiencing drug use, academic failure, and run-ins with the law. But does he have ADHD? What do you think?

Paul may very well have an attention deficit disorder, but the case study does not provide enough evidence to support this diagnosis. Unfortunately, this situation is all too common. The older a student becomes, the harder it is to accurately diagnose them if they have ADHD. Remember, the fundamental characteristics of ADHD do not tend to go away over time; instead, they manifest themselves in different forms. For example, by the time students like Paul reach middle school, they have learned to mask their inattention, hyperactivity, or impulsivity by acting "tough" or "cool." Further, with the increased risk of drug use, it is likely that parents and teachers will believe that inappropriate behavior is the result of being high and not from an underlying disorder.

What Other Conditions Are Likely to Explain Paul's Behavior?

If Paul doesn't have ADHD, what could be causing his behavior? The possibilities are endless. However, two possible explanations appear plausible.

The first is that Paul is "experimenting" with drugs more than he is admitting. The effects of alcoholism and drug addition can make people act just like Paul—defensive, moody, unmotivated, and hostile. Given the information provided in the case study, this is a possibility that you should address even without additional evidence.

The second possibility is that Paul is going through a tough time and doesn't know how to express himself. Adolescence can be a very challenging time. Everything is changing. You feel like an adult, but nobody treats you like one. It can be very easy for some students to rebel in unproductive ways, such as with Paul. But just because this may be common, it doesn't mean that you can't help Paul. So what would you do?

Adolescents tend to need three things. The first is increased self-esteem. People who feel good about themselves usually don't feel the need to take drugs. Further, if Paul felt that he could do well in academic subjects, he probably would show up for class.

Second, adolescents need to feel more independent. They have the bodies of adults, but are often treated as children. This is not to say that adolescents should be living on their own, but without experiencing increased independence, they will never be ready for what the adult world has in store for them.

Finally, adolescents want control. They need to know that they have some control over their lives. They have to see that they can make some of their own decisions and their own mistakes. This is part of growing up.

How Could You Increase Paul's Self-Esteem?

One method of improving people's self-esteem is to give them opportunities to succeed. The trick with Paul is that he needs to succeed in academic subjects that he refuses to attend. So how can you get him to attend math, science, and English?

One way of reaching Paul is through his art. If you can somehow tie his interests in art to academic subjects, he might be more motivated to attend classes. Perhaps you could have him enroll in an art history class, or perhaps you could have him enroll in a poetry class with the notion that learning about poetry would help him become a better lyricist. Further, if he likes art, he might also like drafting, which involves math and science. Drafting might also give him a "fall-back" career should music not work out for him.

How Could You Increase Paul's Independence and Control?

Paul's behavior seems to stem from his desire to gain control over his life. No matter how much he likes the idea of an art history class, he is likely to reject it if he feels that you and his parents are making him do it. Consequently, you might help guide Paul so that he can make his own decisions. Giving him options might also be valuable.

The issue of most concern regarding Paul is his drug use. Although it is unclear how extensively he has used drugs, a pre-intervention certainly is warranted. There are several good ways of educating students about the dangers of drugs. One is to have him talk to peers who have been addicts. By listening to their stories, Paul may decide to alter his behavior. Further, by allowing Paul to gain control of his life, he may determine that he no longer needs drugs to feel good about himself.

CHAPTER 8

Strategies for Adults with ADHD

CHAPTER OBJECTIVES

This chapter answers the following questions:

1. What is ADHD like during adulthood?
2. How can you prepare students for continuing education and employment?
3. How can you prepare students for marriage and intimacy?

CASE STUDY: CANDACE

I have a friend who needs some serious help. Let's call her "Candace." Candace complains constantly about everything. If she is not complaining that she has no social life, she is complaining that she is too busy for one. Further, she can be rather intense as far as relationships go. When she does go out with somebody, she gets very serious about him after just a couple dates. As a result, she rarely has a steady boyfriend.

It is not that I don't like Candace. I do. In fact, we go out two or three times a month. But sometimes it is very hard to be around her for any length of time. Everything is a big production with her. She is always at least an hour late to everything. What is worse, she feels it necessary to tell you exactly why she is late. She will tell you every little detail, no matter how pointless. Most of the time, she just rambles on and on.

Further, watching Candace around her apartment should be a television sitcom. First of all, it is absolutely filthy. Clothes, dirty and "clean," are thrown about the bedroom. Books are scattered about the living room. In the kitchen, utensils are stuck to the dirty counter tops. Additionally, Candace will spend an hour running around her apartment trying to find something only to forget what she was looking for.

The really sad thing about Candace is that, even though she can be a scatterbrain, she is actually really bright. She is very good at finding creative solutions to difficult problems and seeing things in a unique light. I guess she tried going to college, but dropped out of two different universities due to poor grades. Apparently, she had difficulty even graduating high school.

Her behavior has hurt Candace professionally as well as socially. She has had seven jobs over the past three years—three of which she was fired from. Initially, Candace liked all seven positions. After a couple of weeks, however, she became bored with her duties and decided that she didn't like her coworkers.

As Candace always says, her life is a mess. Unfortunately, she just doesn't seem to understand why or how to make it better.

Case Study Questions

1. Do you think Candace has ADHD? Explain.
2. Other than ADHD, what could be causing Candace's difficulties?
3. How could you help Candace with her job or continuing education?
4. How could you help Candace with relationships?

WHAT IS ADHD LIKE DURING ADULTHOOD?

Adults with ADHD have certain characteristics that are unlike younger individuals. While some studies have found that ADHD-symptoms decrease slightly with age (Hallowell and Ratey 1994; Weiss 1992), most experts agree that the adults with ADHD still have considerable problems adjusting to a non-ADHD world (Hallowell 1993; Nadeau 1994; Weiss and Hechtman 1986). For example, they often have problems with employment, continuing education, marriage, and daily functioning (Murphy 1992).

Consider for a moment these statistics from Weiss and Hechtman (1986): Over 30 percent of your students with ADHD will never complete high school. Less than 5 percent of your students with ADHD will earn a bachelor's degree from a university. Further, when your students become adults, they are more likely to become addicted to illegal and prescription drugs, alcohol, food, compulsive shopping, overworking, and excessive gambling than non-ADHD adults (Wender 1987). Finally, 75 percent of adults with ADHD complain of chronic interpersonal problems, especially with their significant others.

Employment, marriage, and continuing education are three areas of concern for adults with ADHD. For example, adults with ADHD change jobs frequently because they become bored with their assigned duties and coworkers. Further, their distractibility, disorganization, antisocial personalities, and inattentiveness contribute to high levels of involuntary job loss.

Adults with ADHD experience increased rates of divorce and unsuccessful relationships (Nadeau 1994; Weiss 1992). Partners commonly complain that adults with ADHD are unable to maintain attention long enough to enjoy sexual activity (Hallowell and Ratey 1994). Further, adults with ADHD often lack the communication skills necessary to build healthy relationships.

Continuing education, employment, and adult relationships are key components of any adult lifestyle. Picture for a moment what your life would be like today if you had dropped out of high school or didn't complete your college degree. What would be your employment potential? How about if you change jobs every three or four months? Do you think you would move up the company ladder very quickly? And what about your relationships? How successful would they be if you couldn't relate to other people, effectively communicate your needs, or enjoy sexual intimacy?

Whether as a parent or a teacher, you will need to prepare your students for adult life. That is the purpose of education. This means more than teaching them reading, writing, and arithmetic. You must prepare them for the transition to the adult world. To do this, you will need to help them explore careers that match their abilities and interests. You will also have to give them skills to develop and maintain personal relationships. Finally, you need to educate them and their families as to the difficulties that they might face later in life, such as drug and alcohol addiction. By preparing your students early on, even as early as preschool, they will be better able to develop into successful adults.

HOW CAN YOU PREPARE STUDENTS
FOR CONTINUING EDUCATION AND EMPLOYMENT?

Adults with ADHD tend to be bright, creative, and energetic. Unfortunately, they also tend not to fulfill their potential. Part of the explanation for this is that few students with ADHD complete college. Nowadays, without a college education, few people can excel professionally.

Another explanation for the lack of success that adults with ADHD experience is that they have the same problems at work as they did when attending school. Employees with ADHD tend to defy authority, become impatient with other people, perform inconsistently, and are disorganized. In short, adults with ADHD have certain gifts; however, in order for these gifts to be utilized, they must be in positions that match their strengths and interests and that minimize their weaknesses.

Accommodations at Schools

One reason why so many students with ADHD drop out of college or never obtain their degree is that they no longer receive the support they got in high school. There are no IEPs in college, nor are there interdisciplinary teams or meetings. College students are fundamentally on their own once they have graduated from high school.

Another reason why students with ADHD tend to have poor experiences in college is that they are unaware of the resources available to them. For example, they do not know that they can get accommodations, such as note takers or extended time on exams. Further, they don't use learning centers or writing clinics. In order to help your students succeed at college, you should invite university representatives to your students' IEP meetings. These university representatives can help your students make the transition to the college environment by informing them of available services and resources on campus. Further, university personal could help lessen the fear that many adults with ADHD have about academic endeavors.

Supports at School

In addition to formal accommodations and learning centers, there are many other sources of assistance at college. For example, colleges tend to have support groups for students with learning disabilities. Befriending peers with ADHD who are succeeding in school might help your students adjust to the demands that college life brings.

Further, departments in psychology or special education can also help students with ADHD. Psychology departments often provide low-cost or free counseling. Special education departments have expertise in curricula modifications useful at the college level. These resources are available at most schools; however, you must empower your students to advocate for themselves. Once they leave high school, they will be their own IEP coordinators.

Finding Career Matches

Did you have a lot of different majors before you went into education? How did you determine that education was what you wanted to do? Adults with ADHD have to find their place in the work world just as you have done. So how do you help students find their niche?

There are several methods of finding the right career. Career counselors can help students determine what they are looking for in a job. There are also aptitude tests and interest inventories that can help reveal your students' strengths, weaknesses, and areas of interest. Some of these include:

* Reading Free Vocational Interest Inventory (RFVII) (Becker, Schull, and Cambell 1981)
* Strong-Campbell Interest Inventory (Campbell and Hansen 1981)
* Self-Directed Search (Form E) (Holland 1985)
* Vocational Interest and Sophistication Assessment (VISA) (Parnicky, Kahn, and Burdett 1971)
* Vocational Profile (Callahan and Garner 1997)
* Woodcock-Johnson Psycho-Educational Battery, Part Three— Tests of Interests (Woodcock and Johnson 1977)

In addition to counseling, aptitude tests, and interest inventories, your students can find the career that best suits them through experimentation. Encourage them to take different jobs each summer. Have them experience diverse professions. Have them take courses in numerous fields of study. Sometimes, the only way that people know they like something is if they try it.

One final thought. There is no one perfect job for everybody. You might like teaching because it allows you to work with people. Others might like computers because they enjoy focusing on details. Although no one career is right for everybody, there are certain vocational characteristics that might help adults with ADHD succeed in the work world.

For instance, adults with ADHD might benefit from positions that offer variability, such as teaching. Teachers get up in front of the classroom presenting information, they grade papers, they work with students one-on-one, they go to meetings, and fill out paperwork. The duties of teachers are very diverse and, consequently, might keep the attention of adults with ADHD.

Good careers for adults with ADHD tend to be active. They involve movement and activity. Do you think a writer or a researcher would be a good position for somebody with ADHD? Maybe. Even though writers and researchers spend considerable time sitting in front of computers, typing may be active enough for some adults with ADHD.

Finally, good careers for adult with ADHD tend to be self-directed. In these positions, workers are able to go at their own pace and be their own bosses. Owning a business is a perfect example of being self-directed. Although business owners frequently put in numerous hours, they can often decide what they are going to do and when.

Accommodations at Work

Once a position is identified, adults with ADHD may wish to increase the likelihood of their success by asking for various accommodations. For example, adults with ADHD could use frequent breaks or an office with a window or with lights that are not fluorescent. Further, workers with ADHD may benefit from flex time where, if they feel too hyper to concentrate, they can take off of work and then make the time up when they are better able to focus.

HOW CAN YOU HELP PREPARE STUDENTS FOR MARRIAGE AND INTIMACY?

This may be hard for an adult without ADHD to understand, but certain activities can be considered "mentally painful" for adults with ADHD. For instance, have you ever been trapped in a very small place and you wanted to get out at any cost? Do you remember that intense anxiety that you felt when your movements were restricted or you thought the air was running out? Adults with ADHD experience that type of feeling during what you might consider routine behaviors.

For example, a simple hug might be difficult to endure for an adult with ADHD. The same is true for snuggling with a partner. Even a gentle caress could produce a sense of anxiety within an adult with ADHD, especially those who are in a hyperactive cycle.

Further, individuals with ADHD have great difficulty regulating their energy level. They are either going as fast as they can or they are completely dead in their tracks. One moment an adult can be actively interacting with their partner, the next they can be withdrawn and exhausted. This can be a source of tremendous frustration to their partners, who never know when the next "on" cycle will begin.

Throughout the lives of individuals with ADHD, social skills tend to be underdeveloped. They frequently have difficult controlling their emotions as well as understanding other people's point of view. They also have problems expressing their emotions appropriately and communicating their needs to significant others. Additionally, partners of adults with ADHD often lack an understanding of ADHD and do not know how to address issues that might be related to the condition. There are several ways that you can help.

Premarital Classes

Premarital classes can help any couple gain a better understanding of each other's needs. They can be particularly helpful for individuals who have ADHD and are not well skilled in the art of communication. In addition to enhancing communication skills, premarital classes help couples ask questions that they otherwise would have not thought about asking, thus building a stronger relationship.

Open Communication

The importance of open communication that premarital classes and other strategies can foster cannot be underestimated. Frequently, both partners harbor anger or resentment toward each other due to misunderstandings and differing expectations of behavior. Being able to talk about these feelings can help couples navigate through rough times.

Educating Partners about ADHD

As with parents, siblings, and educators, partners of adults with ADHD need to understand the condition. They need to know how to address issues relating to hyperactivity, impulsivity, and inappropriate social skills. Without this understanding, partners may experience frustration as a result of their loved ones' erratic and unorthodox behaviors.

There are several ways to help educate partners of adults with ADHD. For instance, encourage them to go to support groups or meetings of

ADHD organizations (e.g., CHADD). Suggest books and articles that describe ADHD in nontechnical terms, or have them talk with other partners of adults with ADHD. Chapter 10 contains a list of resources, such as books, Web sites, and support groups that can help partners of adults with ADHD understand attention deficit hyperactivity disorders.

FORMING A SUPPORT GROUP

No matter how good a person or teacher you are, or how knowledgeable, there will be times when people learn more from their peers than they learn from you. Let's face it: What you know about ADHD most likely comes from books, your college courses, and through observing your students. Unless you actually have ADHD, your knowledge is rather limited. It is like trying to explain to a mother what it is like to give birth when you have never had a baby yourself. You can quote statistics and share your observations, but in many ways, you have no idea what you are talking about. It is for this reason why support groups are so important and effective.

There are several national organizations and support groups for individuals with ADHD and their families (see chapter 10). There are probably local and state chapters of these groups within your community. However, you may wish to help your students or their parents form a support group of their own. Here are several ways you can get them started:

- Host regularly occurring get-togethers or workshops for the family members of your students. Allow time for participants to socialize and get to know each other.
- Start a newsletter and solicit help from students and parents. Perhaps they could share tips and resources on ADHD with their readers.
- If a student or parent has a question or problem, refer them to a family who has experienced a similar situation. However, make sure you have the family's permission before you give out their names and phone number.
- Build linkages to other schools and grade levels. For instance, if you teach at the middle school level, invite parents of student who are currently in elementary school to your functions. Further, when a student is about to move on to high school, have them meet other high school students and teachers.
- Allow parents and students to take the lead role in the development and maintenance of support groups. After all, it is their group, not yours.

Focusing on Intent, Not Behavior

Have you ever been with somebody who frequently said things that started out as a compliment but ended up as an insult? For example, a student might tell you that you were a better teacher that she thought you would be, or that you were smarter than you act. Such comments are easily misinterpreted and might cause ill feelings with partners of ADHD.

In order for couples to develop healthy relationships, they must be able to overlook such slips of the tongue. Further, they need to understand that their partner's inattention does not necessarily reflect on them. In other words, partners of adults with ADHD must try to focus on the intent of their significant others, and not their actual behaviors.

Planning Sexual Activities

It is often said that spontaneity spices up a couple's love live. Although this may be true, good planning may help adults with ADHD discover when sexual behavior is most plausible. In other words, couples need to determine the best time for intimacy. For example, adults with ADHD might come home from work emotionally and physically exhausted. Conversely, there may be times when an individual is too hyperactive to focus on sex. Understanding when these times occur will help couples plan for intimacy.

APPLYING WHAT YOU HAVE LEARNED

ADHD does not go away once your students leave high school. In fact, attention disorders present entirely different problems for adults than for children and adolescents. For example, without the support from special education programs, adults with disabilities tend to have a more difficult time in college than they did in high school. Further, people with ADHD frequently have problems with adult relationships and employer's expectations. It is for these reasons you will need to prepare your students for adult life. The sooner this preparation begins, the better.

Reread the case study of Candace at the beginning of the chapter. Do you think that she has ADHD? If she doesn't have ADHD, what could be causing her difficulties? How could you help Candace succeed in college or employment? How would you help her develop healthy adult relationships?

Does Candace Have ADHD?

You probably know people like Candace, people whose lives are always in chaos and upheaval. Do you think that they, and Candace, have ADHD? If so, what type?

In Candace's case, she seems like a prime candidate for an attention disorder. Did you identify some of the key symptoms? For example, she loses things; she is forgetful, disorganized, and distractible; she talks excessively; she moves from job to job; and she appears to be rather restless. It is possible that she would meet the criteria for ADHD-C, especially if these behaviors were present during childhood.

What Else Could Be Causing Candace's Behavior?

No matter how clear it is to you that somebody has ADHD, you should always consider other possibilities. Never rush into a diagnosis. For example, other than ADHD, what could be causing Candace difficulties?

The most obvious alternative is that Candace has a great deal on her mind. Perhaps her social or employment problems are consuming her thoughts. As a result, she comes across as inattentive and distractible. The question that needs to be answered is, "Was Candace like this when she was a child?" If she was, the argument for a diagnosis of ADHD is strengthened. If her behavior is recent, her problems are likely to be caused by situational factors, such as displeasure with her life.

How Could You Help Candace Succeed in College or Employment?

Suppose that you were Candace's teacher. It doesn't matter whether you taught her during first grade or twelfth. How could you help her succeed academically or professionally?

One way to help Candace is to teach her how advocate for herself. This would benefit her tremendously throughout her life, especially in college and at work. After leaving high school, Candace will have to negotiate with professors and employers for accommodations that could help her be a better student and worker. Having her practice these negotiation skills in your classroom would be a good start.

In addition, you will need to help Candace learn more about her strengths, weaknesses, and interests. After understanding these, she will be better able to find an appropriate college and employer. Further, if she possesses strong self-advocacy skills, Candace will know what she wants and how to get it.

How Would You Help Candace
Develop Healthy Adult Relationships?

A life without relationships can be unfulfilling. For this reason, you should help your students acquire the skills they need to develop and maintain healthy relationships. With this in mind, what skills would you teach her?

In addition to self-advocacy and self-awareness, you might also teach Candace effective communication skills. Further, she will need to be able to control her emotions as well as be able to be empathetic toward other people's feelings. These skills can be taught at any age. Further, they will benefit her throughout her entire life.

CHAPTER 9

Developing, Implementing, and Assessing Educational Programs

CHAPTER OBJECTIVES

This chapter answers the following questions:

1. How do I determine the needs of my students?
2. What are appropriate goals for my students?
3. How do I figure out what motivates my students?
4. How can I help my students reach their goals?
5. How can I tell if the education plans are helping my students?

INTRODUCTION

Suppose that you have a student or child with ADHD. You go through this text, select a few ways to modify the classroom and home environments, determine methods of enhancing your teaching, and identify strategies for teaching lifelong skills. Are you finished? Not by a long shot.

Picture yourself trying to paint a scale picture of some beautiful architecture, such as the Eiffel Tower, the Brandenburg Gate, or the Brooklyn Bridge. But instead of measuring the angles and taking into consideration depth perception, you simply begin flinging paint onto the canvass like mashed potatoes at your little brother. Unfortunately, this is how many people teach.

Teaching is an art form as well as a science. Painting without concern for angles or perception may produce a beautiful picture. However, teaching without measurement or concern for a student's current level of abilities can be considered "educational malpractice." It is immensely important that you determine your students' needs as well as whether your strategies are helping them accomplish their goals.

HOW DO I DETERMINE THE NEEDS OF MY STUDENTS?

Before you begin working with a student, you must first determine what you should teach. One way of beginning this process is to determine what a "typical" student will need to know in order to advance to the next grade. For example, suppose that you have a third grader with ADHD. You can examine the fourth grade curriculum and ask the fourth grade teachers what prerequisite skills are needed for students to succeed in their classes. This information gives you a rough idea of what your student will need to learn during third grade. But how about behavior? How do you determine what behaviors you should teach your students?

Identifying the Behavioral Needs of Your Students

Ideally, all students should be able to sit quietly in their desks and raise their hands when they have something to say, but this not how children behave in the real world. So how do you know when your hyperactive child is behaving like a typical kid? When is horseplay developmentally appropriate and when is it caused by ADHD? How many times can a student get out of her chair without being "hyperactive?" How do you know if your students need to work on their attention or social skills?

These are very tough questions. Unfortunately, there are no easy answers to them. However, there are several points that you should keep in mind when you work with students who are different from what is perceived as "typical."

What Has Been Tried in the Past?

First, teachers often see the diagnosis "ADHD" in a student's file and they automatically assume that the student should have goals focusing on attention or social skills. These teachers never make an effort to determine whether the student's actual behavior is better or worse than that of their peers. Think about it. Do you believe that every person diagnosed with ADHD needs to work on attention or social skills? If their elementary school teachers were effective, high school students with ADHD should already have the abilities needed to act appropriately as well the skills needed to maximize their attention.

Whose Goals Are They?

Second, these are not your goals; they are the students'. You should not be the one who determines what your students' needs are. That is up to the student and the IEP team as a whole. Remember, when you walk into an IEP meeting, you are part of a team. Teachers know education. Parents know their child. But in order to help the students, all team members have to work together.

Helping the IEP Team Determine Annual Goals

How do you help students and the rest of the IEP team formulate annual goals? Ask your students what they would like to work on. If they don't have any ideas, help them picture where they see themselves in five, ten, or twenty years. If they see college in the picture, brainstorm a list of skills that the student will need in order to complete a degree. If they see a marriage, determine what communication skills would help him or her develop a loving, nurturing relationship.

There are no pat answers. There are no cookie-cutter solutions. There are no lists of what to do when a student has such-and-such disability and has such-and-such characteristics. Listen, observe, and ask questions—lots of questions. That is how you determine the needs of your students.

Why Focus on "Typical" Students?

There is one last thing to keep in mind when determining the needs of your students. Why focus on what "typical" students can or can't do? What does it matter? If you have a student who can't read, teach her to read. If a student has self-abusive behaviors, get him to stop. If a fifth grader can do college trigonometry, then teach her to do trigonometry at a graduate school level.

Suppose you are teaching a student vocational skills at a restaurant. At the grill next to your student works a "typical" student without

ADHD. The typical student sneezes on a piece of meat, puts it in a bun, and sends it to the customer's table. Is this how you want your student with ADHD to behave?

Whether you are a teacher or a parent, it is probably your goal to help your students to become whatever or whoever they want to become. It doesn't matter what his or her peers are doing. Do as much as you can with your students in the time that you have. That is what teaching is all about.

WHAT ARE APPROPRIATE GOALS FOR MY STUDENTS?

You have met with your students, talked at length with their family members, and gathered all kinds of diverse information. They have given you good ideas of what your students' needs are, but how do you determine what goals are appropriate? Again, there are no clear answers. However, consider these scenarios.

A Few Students and Their Goals

Suppose that you have a student with severe ADHD-C. He can barely touch a seat before jumping up again. He is behind his grade level in nearly every subject, he rarely pays attention, and IQ tests indicate that he has below average intelligence. Despite all of this, this student's parents indicate that they want their child to go to college and become a world-renowned physicist. Do you think that is an appropriate goal for this student?

Suppose you have another student who is so socially awkward that it is difficult to be near him without laughing or groaning at him in embarrassment. On the infrequent occasions when you can actually understand what he says, he is completely inappropriate. Further, he has mood swings that range from elation to deep depression, he has difficulty paying attention to other people, and would lose his head if it were not attached to his body. Still, this student wants to be a lawyer or a politician. Is this an appropriate goal for this student?

One more example. Suppose that you had a student who was the stereotypical troublemaker. He gets into fights, drinks before and after school, never finishes what he starts, and although he loves to read, he refuses to read books for school or complete assignments. In his IEP meeting, he says that he wants to be a rock 'n' roll star—even though he admits that he can't read music or sing very well. Is this an appropriate goal for this student?

It is very tempting to look at students and say, "That's a nice dream that you have, but it wouldn't make an appropriate goal" or "That's not realistic." Think about the three students about which you just read. Were you tempted to say something negative about their goals? Perhaps you were ready to suggest an alternative goal, "just in case you don't make it as a rock star."

The truth is, the first student is very similar to Albert Einstein. Did you know that he was considered "slow" as a child? In fact, he failed science and mathematics. It wasn't until later in his life that he was recognized as a genius.

The second student resembles Abraham Lincoln. He suffered from severe depression and was painfully shy. There are stories that he would frequently forget things at people's houses but he did not have the courage to ask for them back. Moreover, his poor memory was legendary. His wife had to follow him around the White House picking up things so that he wouldn't lose them.

The third student is much like John Lennon. Though obviously a bright child, John Lennon refused to complete schoolwork and barely graduated from high school. He was argumentative, insubordinate, and had a problem managing his anger. He drank, he fought, and he went out of his way to give his teachers a difficult time. However, when his teachers told him that he would never become a rock star, Lennon proved them wrong.

Don't Be Too Quick to Deny Students Their Dreams

What is the moral of the story? If a guy named Albert wants to be a scientist, let him? Not quite. The moral is not to be too quick to say that something is "inappropriate" or "unrealistic." If your third grader wants to be an astronaut or movie star, help her prepare to become an astronaut or a movie star. Chances are, the skills that the student will need to be an astronaut or movie star will help her become many other things as well.

How Difficult Should Goals Be to Achieve?

You are probably thinking, "Okay, I will let my students dream. In fact, I will help them anyway that I can to obtain those dreams. But I have no idea how hard or easy to make my students' annual goals." There are two philosophies that you should consider when determining the difficulty level of goals that you are setting for your students.

Some people think you should "reach for the stars." By that, they mean goals should be set very high—even if the students probably won't accomplish them. High goals are thought to show students what is expected of them as well as prepare them for life's challenges.

Others believe that goals should be set just within their students' reach. The idea being that success is a powerful motivator and that once a goal is met, a new goal can be devised. In effect, these smaller goals build upon each other to form the same goal proposed by those who "reach for the stars."

Both philosophies have their advocates and critics. For example, suppose that you have a professor who gives easy quizzes every week. The quizzes are so easy that you barely need to open your book to get an A. Suppose that you have another professor who only gives an extremely hard final exam. It is so hard that half the class usually fails it and, subsequently, fails the class. Which professor's style do you like better?

Some people might prefer the hard final exam because it is a challenge to overcome. Further, these people might feel bored or understimulated by the series of easy quizzes. As a result, they might become discouraged with the class and not learn as much had they been given greater challenges. Other people might become so afraid of taking the very hard final exam that they give up before they even try. See the point?

If you need some sort of definite answer, then try this. The best IEP goal is probably some where in between the stars and your students' reach; where exactly depends on the needs of your students and how they are motivated.

HOW DO I FIGURE OUT WHAT MOTIVATES MY STUDENTS?

Motivation is the foundation upon which successful teaching is built. Suppose for the moment that you have a professor who teaches the history of special education, hundreds of definitions, and many different theories of human behavior. However, she doesn't teach anything that you believe will actually help you be a better educator. How motivated would you be to learn in her class?

Talking with Your Students

Have you ever had students ask you "Why do we need to know this stuff?" What did you say? "Because I said so?" If you can't answer their questions and convince them that what you are teaching is important for their futures, they won't be motivated to learn. However, even if you can convince your students that algebra or chemistry is important to their futures, they may not care. You will need to determine how to reach each individual student. How do you do that?

The simplest way to determine what motivates students is to ask them. Remember, education involves more than just you. It involves your students and their family members. One of the most effective strategies that you can use as a teacher or parent is to sit down with students and negotiate with them. Tell them what you expect and propose a suitable reward. Allow your students to counteroffer until you both reach an agreement. For example, if your inattentive student turns in her homework on time, she might get a piece of candy for lunch. Now just imagine if you tried to reinforce positive behavior with candy and the student didn't like sweets! Would you motivate her?

Why Do Your Students Behave the Way They Do?

Determining what your students would like for a reward is only part of the motivation picture. You'll also have to figure out why your students are behaving in a certain way, such as throwing objects across the room or showing up to class late. In other words, you'll have to ask yourself, "What is compelling my students to do that?"

Most behaviors that your students will do will be the result of three possibilities. First, your students are trying to get something that they want, such as attention. Second, they are trying to avoid something that they don't want, such as looking stupid in front of their peers. Third, they are behaving a certain way because they are trying to get something as well as avoid something, such as getting respect from their peers and avoid doing work.

Usually, students will not tell you why they are acting inappropriately; perhaps they do not know. In order to figure out what is motivating a student to misbehave, you have to become a detective.

For example, suppose you have a student who mimics everything you say. You have tried numerous strategies to get him to stop. You have had him sign behavioral contracts, taken away privileges, rewarded positive behavior when it occurs, you have even tried satiating the behavior by ignoring his mimicking everything that is said all day long—but nothing seems to work. Any idea why you have been unsuccessful? A good start is to figure out what he was getting or avoiding when mimicking you.

Try this one. Suppose that a student of yours frequently uses profanity. Every time things don't go his way, he becomes very upset and starts cussing like a drunken sailor. He'll swear at you, other children, and even objects. The student has been suspended, put in time out, tokens have been taken away—nothing seems to compel him to watch his language. Why do you think he is swearing?

One more example. This is a bit harder. Suppose that a student keeps getting out of her seat without permission. You have threatened her. You have begged her. You have tried everything short of putting locking seat belts on her chair, and although she always apologizes for getting up, nothing seems to keep her seated. Why is she getting out of her chair?

Think about your three students described briefly above. Why are they acting the way they do? What is motivating them to face punishment, pass up rewards, and endure your wrath? Only when you can answer these questions with some degree of certainty will you be able to effectively teach these students.

Let's take a look at the first student. What is he trying to get or avoid when he mimics what you say? You'll never truly know for sure, but there are several possibilities. For example, this student could be trying to get you angry. One way to attempt to determine whether the student is trying to avoid work is to examine when he is misbehaving. If he acts out primarily when you are about to begin topics that are difficult for him, it would seem that your theory might be correct.

The student might also be trying to make his peers laugh, thus getting their attention as well as respect. However, if the student keeps mimicking you when no students are around, then this theory doesn't appear to fit the facts.

Let's try the second student. Why is this student swearing all the time? Is it to get a bad reputation so that other students think he's cool? Is he trying to get out of class? Is he trying to avoid looking stupid when things go wrong? Again, you have to look at the facts. If this student swears when no other students are present, influencing his peers might not be the primary reason for his behavior—it might be part of the overall picture, but not the key. Is there any pattern to when he swears, such as during certain subjects or when certain people are around? How does he act when he is swearing? Does it seem as if he wants to leave the room, or do the words just come out of his mouth without his realizing it?

How about the last student? Why does she get out of her seat all of the time? Is she trying to get supplies or to socialize with a peer? Does she get out of her seat at any particular part of the day, such as before lunch or after gym?

Do you see how you can develop a theory as to why students are behaving inappropriately and then gather information to help determine whether this theory is correct? Once you determine what your students are trying to avoid or get, you can better address their behavior. For example, if a student is acting out to get attention, you should prevent the behavior by giving him what he wants (e.g., attention from his peers) for *proper* behavior.

Sound easy? Well, there is one more hitch. Not all behaviors can be explained by getting something or avoiding something. Go back and read about the first student, the one who repeats everything you say. What if that student has echolalia? Does that change your assessment of why the student is acting that way? How about the second student? What if he had Tourette's syndrome? Would you still punish him if he swears? And what if the student who can't stay in her seat has ADHD-HI? Hopefully, you have learned by now that making hyperactive students sit down when they just can't is a battle best avoided.

In summary, when teaching your students, you must be able to motivate them. In order to motivate them, you must understand what they find reinforcing. For example, praise from a teacher or parent might motivate one student while being a punishment for another student. Further, when your students misbehave, you must be able to develop potential explanations as to why they are acting inappropriately. But take care, sometime troubling behaviors are caused by medical or biological factors, not by the students themselves.

REINFORCING APPROPRIATE BEHAVIOR

Rewarding students for their appropriate behavior is the best strategy that parents and teachers can use. This probably sounds like common sense, but it is not as easy as it seems. For example, suppose you are walking around your classroom watching your students complete some individual seat work and you notice that your student with ADHD is actually on task! What do you do? Do you praise her? Give her a sticker? Put a check mark by her name?

Rewarding students while they are on task can be the worst thing that you could do. Think about it. Remember when you pictured somebody interrupting your reading and you had difficulty getting back on task? Same thing here. By rewarding a student who is on task, you are actually taking her off task.

The best thing to do is to reward your students as they are beginning to get off task. Give them some encouragement. Help them realize their success and then guide them back to the task at hand, or reward students when the task is over.

However, sometimes it is difficult to know how to reward students. What is rewarding to one student might actually be a punishment to others. Consider the use of praise or attention. Do your like students always like attention? Do you remember prom night? Did your parents come running out of the house with their cameras blasting away saying how cute you looked? Kind of embarrassing, wasn't it? Now picture yourself as a teenager who is trying to fit in and be "cool." Having a teacher make a big fuss that you completed an assignment doesn't help you maintain that image. Monitor the amount of enthusiasm with which you try to reward your students. Sometimes a subtle "good job," "I'm proud of you," or a thumb's up is the best reinforcement.

Finally, you don't want to give students so much reinforcement that it loses its meaning. Have you ever had a friend who compliments you on what you are wearing? No matter what you wear, he says, "You look great in that!" Even if you are just in old sweat pants and a T-shirt, he just raves about your fashion sense. After a while, does his opinion really matter much?

The same can happen with your students. Imagine if you were a student and your teacher rewarded you every time you handed something in, even if you got a C-. Think of reinforcement like a dessert. They are best when you have them once in a while and not for every meal. Plus, they are only desserts if you like them.

HOW CAN I HELP MY STUDENTS REACH THEIR GOALS?

Once you have determined the needs of your students and developed a theory as to what motivates them, the next step is help them reach their goals. But how do you do this?

Remediating a Problem

Suppose that your students' goals are directed at remediating a problem, such as low reading or math scores. When developing strategies to help these students, you first need to examine the root causes for why the students are having difficulties. Many times the root cause is related to being hyperactive, inattentive, or some other characteristic of ADHD. If this is the case, you could use the strategies listed throughout this text.

What if you are not sure why your students are behind in math or reading? How do you develop strategies that can help them accomplish their goals? First, examine the students' records and past IEPs. What types of strategies have been utilized in the past? Try developing something new. Moreover, try multiple strategies, such as peer teaching, manipulatives, computer software, and rewarding improvement. The more things that you try, the more likely you will find what works for that student.

Second, ask the students why they think they are having problems. Have them be honest. Were they bored by their past teachers? Do they feel frustrated from failure and, therefore, do not want to try? When do they feel most able to learn? When is learning most difficult? If they could be taught any way they wanted, what would that way be like?

Students can often help you determine what their primary learning styles are. For example, ask them if it is easier to remember a phone number if they see it, hear it, or if they dial it; or ask them if they are more likely to remember how to get to a friend's house if they are told the directions, see a map, or drive there once. This can help you determine if your students are visual, auditory, or kinetic learners. This information is a good starting point for developing strategies.

Working with New Problems

What if your students have goals that do not involve skills that they have worked on before? For example, imagine that you have a student, Bill, who just turned twelve years old and he is starting to become very interested in sexuality. Unfortunately, instead of asking girls out, he pats them on their butt and makes inappropriate sexual remarks. What do you do?

Suppose that you, Bill, and Bill's parents all agree that Bill needs to learn how to interact with women more appropriately. Further, you think that you have determined the two primary forces motivating Bill to act inappropriately. First, grabbing a woman's butt is the closest that Bill has come to kissing or being sexually active with a female. You assume that when Bill touches a girl, he obtains a feeling of sexual arousal he hasn't previously experienced.

Second, by making sexually inappropriate comments, Bill is in a way avoiding rejection. Think of it this way. If Bill were to try to approach a girl and ask her out, she might laugh at him and say "no." However, if he acts like a jerk, he knows that they will say "no" and he can pretend that he didn't care.

Lastly, you believe that Bill needs to increase his confidence as well as obtain suitable social skills. One way of increasing confidence is to set some of his goals low enough so that he experiences success. So you develop goals using the "within his reach" philosophy.

Okay. How do you develop strategies for Bill's new behaviors? No strategies have been utilized in the past, so you have to begin brand new.

Let's look at the facts. Bill is touching girls and saying sexually inappropriate things because he doesn't know how else to interact with them. Further, Bill is trying to obtain sexual gratification as well as to protect himself from being rejected. Whatever strategies you develop must teach Bill social skills that help him manage potential rejection. You must also eliminate what is rewarding Bill's inappropriate behavior, especially the sexual gratification.

What strategies have you come up with? You might develop some strategies involving peer teaching. Remember the strategy discussed earlier—the one involving female high school students and how they expect guys to behave. Perhaps you could use the same strategy with Bill. For example, get a group of responsible females students to role-play acceptable behavior with Bill, such as practicing asking girls out. Further, in class, you might give Bill opportunities to work in groups with female students. Additionally, if Bill does not act appropriately toward females, his role-playing with female high school students, which is most likely a reinforcement, can be revoked.

HOW CAN I TELL IF THE
EDUCATION PLANS ARE HELPING MY STUDENTS?

You have just developed strategies for your students; now what do you do? If you are an effective teacher or parent, you will see whether your strategies are working.

Collecting Data

Before you begin any strategy, you need to collect information on the behaviors that you are trying to increase or decrease. This is often

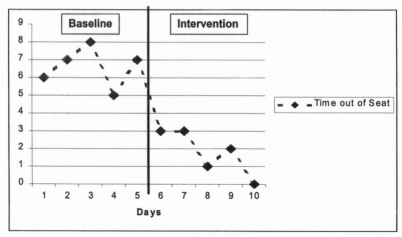

Figure 9.1   *A Sample Graph of a Student's Out-of-Seat Behavior.*

called "baseline data." In the case of Bill discussed above, you would need to determine how frequently he touches females and how often he makes inappropriate sexual comments.

Once you begin using your strategies or "interventions," you will need to keep collecting data on the student's behaviors. It is important that you keep collecting data the same way during the intervention phase as you did during baseline. You need to be consistent.

Examining the Results

Now compare the results. Graphs, such as the one here, really help if you are a visual learner. Did the behavior increase as you wanted? Is there a trend to the behavior? How far does the student have left to go to achieve his goal? By assessing the impact of your strategies on your students' behaviors, you will be able to determine whether or not they are effective. Further, if your strategies are not working, your assessments might help you find out why—thus giving you valuable insight as to what to try next.

SUMMARY

Teaching is not just about presenting information and giving assignments. You are a detective, a scientist, and an artist. As a teacher or parent, you must figure out what your students need to learn. Specifically, you have to determine what academic abilities your students need to obtain so that they can progress to the next grade as well as what behaviors they need to display in order to be successful in life.

You'll also need to know what goals are appropriate for your individual students. Should you set their goals high or low? That all depends on their needs and what motivates them.

Learning what motivates your students will be the most important skill that you can develop as an effective teacher. If you can't motivate your students to learn, you cannot teach them, nor can you develop strategies that suit their needs.

Being a parent or teacher is like tending a garden. Sometimes it takes long time to see the fruits of your labors. Some seasons, it appears as if nothing will grow at all. Further, not all plants are alike. Some require a lot of light; others need a certain type of soil or amount of water. Lastly, many weeds turn out to have beautiful flowers.

How good of a gardener you become will depend upon your willingness to learn new things and to unlearn behaviors that once suited you well. Reading books, such as this one, is one way to keep abreast of new ideas. However, you will gain far more from listening to your students and their family members than from reading any text.

Realize that you have a lot to learn and you always will. You will never stop being a student. Remember too that you are not your students' only teacher. Get to know, and utilize, their peers and other family members. Finally, believe in yourself, your students, and your ability to change the world one child at a time.

ADHD is a gift. Use it, don't repress it!

CHAPTER 10

Resources for Teachers, Parents, and Individuals with ADHD

BOOKS FOR TEACHERS AND OTHER PROFESSIONALS

American Psychiatric Association. 1994. *Diagnostic and Statistical Manual of Mental Disorders.* 4th ed. Washington, D.C.: Author.

Barkley, R. A. 1987. *Defiant Children: A Clinician's Manual for Parent Training.* New York: Guilford Press.

Barkley, R. A. 1990. *Attention-Deficit Hyperactivity Disorder: A Handbook for Diagnosis and Treatment.* New York: Guilford Press.

Bender, W. N. 1997. *Understanding ADHD: A Practical Guide for Teachers and Parents.* Upper Saddle River, N.J.: Prentice Hall.

Copeland, E., and V. Love. 1990. *Attention without Tension: A Teacher's Handbook on Attention Disorders.* Atlanta: 3C's Of Childhood.

Dowdy, C. A., J. R. Patton, T. E. C. Smith, and E. A. Polloway. 1998. *Attention-Deficit/Hyperactivity Disorder in the Classroom: A Practical Guide for Teachers.* Austin, Tex.: PRO-ED.

DuPaul, G. J., and G. Stoner. 1994. *ADHD in the Schools: Assessment and Intervention Strategies.* New York: Guilford Press.

Fowler, M. 1992. *Ch.A.D.D. Educators' Manual: An In-Depth Look at Attention Deficit Disorders from an Educational Perspective.* Plantation, Fla.: Ch.A.D.D.

Hallowell, E .H., and J. J. Ratey. 1994. *Driven to Distraction.* New York: Simon & Schuster.

Lyon, R., and N. Krasnegor. 1996. *Attention, Memory, and Executive Function.* Baltimore, Md.: Brookes.

Mash, E. J., and R. A. Barkley, eds. 1989. *Treatment of Childhood Disorders.* New York: Guilford Press.

Parker, H. 1991. *The ADD-Hyperactivity Handbook for Schools.* Plantation, Fla.: Specialty Press.

Parker, H. 1992. *ADAPT: Attention Deficit Accommodation Plan for Teaching.* Plantation, Fla.: Specialty Press.

Parker, H. C. 1988. *The ADHD Hyperactivity Workbook for Parents, Teachers, and Kids.* Plantation, Fla.: Impact Publication.

Solden, S. 1995. *Women with Attention Deficit Disorder.* Grass Valley, Calif.: Underwood Books.

Wender, P. 1986. *Hyperactive Children Grown-Up.* New York: Guilford.

Wender, P. 1995. *Attention-Deficit Hyperactivity Disorder in Adults.* New York: Oxford University Press.

Werry, J., and M. Aman. 1993. *Practitioners Guide to Psychoactive Drugs for Children and Adolescents.* New York: Plenum Press.

BOOKS FOR PARENTS AND INDIVIDUALS WITH ADHD

Bain, L. 1991. *A Parent's Guide to Attention Deficit Disorder.* New York: Delta/Dell.

Barkley, R. A. 1990. *Attention-Deficit Hyperactivity Disorder: A Handbook for Diagnosis and Treatment.* New York: Guilford Press.

Barkley, R. A. 1995. *Taking Charge of ADHD: The Complete, Authoritative Guide for Parents.* New York: Guilford Press.

Bauer, K. 1993. *Active Andy: An Elementary School Child's Guide to Understanding ADHD.* Wauwatosa, Wis.: IMDW Publishing.

Childworks. 1995. *Sometimes I Drive My Mom Crazy, but I Know She's Crazy about Me!* King of Prussia, Penn.: Center for Applied Psychology, Inc.

Copeland, E., and V. Love. 1991. *Attention, Please: A Comprehensive Guide for Successfully Parenting Children with Attention Disorders and Hyperactivity.* Atlanta: 3Cs of Childhood.

Corman, C., and E. Trevino. 1995. *Eulcee, the Jumpy Jumpy Elephant.* Plantation, Fla.: Specialty Press.

Forgatch, M., and G. R. Patterson. 1989. *Parents and Adolescents Living Together.* Eugene, Ore.: Castalia.

Fowler, M. C. 1990. *Maybe You Know My Kid: A Parent's Guide to Coping with Attention-Deficit Hyperactivity Disorder.* Secaucus, N.J.: Birch Lane.

Galum, M. 1988. *Otto Learns about His Medicine.* New York: Imagination Press.

Gehret, J. 1995. *I'm Somebody Too.* Fairport, N.Y.: Verbal Images Press.

Gehret, J. 1996. *Eagle Eyes: A Child's View of Attention Deficit Disorder.* Fairport, N.Y.: Verbal Images Press.

Goodman, J., and S. Hoban. 1994. *Around the Clock: Parenting the ADHD Child.* New York: Guilford.

Goldstein, S., and M. Goldstein. 1992. *Hyperactivity: Why Won't My Child Pay Attention?* Salt Lake City: Neurology, Learning, and Behavior Center.

Gordon, M. 1991. *ADHD/Hyperactivity: A Consumer's Guide.* Dewitt, N.Y.: GSI.

Gordon, M. 1992. *I Would if I Could.* Dewitt, N.Y.: GSL.

Gordon, M. 1992. *My Brother's a World-Class Pain.* Dewitt, N.Y.: GSL.

Hallowell, E. H., and J. J. Ratey. 1994. *Driven to Distraction.* New York: Simon & Schuster.

Ingersoll, B. 1988. *Your Hyperactive Child: A Parent's Guide to Coping with Attention Deficit Disorder.* New York: Doubleday.

Ingersoll, B., and M. Goldstein. 1993. *Attention Deficit Disorder and Learning Disabilities: Realities, Myths, and Controversial Treatments.* New York: Doubleday.

Johnson, D. 1992. *I Can't Sit Still: Educating and Affirming Inattentive and Hyperactive Children.* Santa Cruz, Calif.: ETR Associates.

Kennedy, P., L. Terdal, and L. Fusetti. 1993. *The Hyperactive Child Book.* New York: St. Martin's Press.

Moss, D. 1989. *Shelly the Hyperactive Turtle.* Rockville, Md.: Woodbine House.

Nadeau, K. G. 1994. *Survival Guide for College Students with ADD or LD.* New York: Magination Press.

Parker, R. 1994. *Making the Grade.* Plantation, Fla.: Specialty Press.

Parker, R. 1995. *Slam Dunk.* Plantation, Fla.: Specialty Press.

Parker, H. C. 1988. *The ADHD Hyperactivity Workbook for Parents, Teachers, and Kids.* Plantation, Fla.: Impact Publication.

Quinn, P. 1994. *ADD and the College Student.* New York: Magination Press.

Solden, S. 1995. *Women with Attention Deficit Disorder.* Grass Valley, Calif.: Underwood Books.

Taylor, J. F. 1990. *Helping Your Hyperactive Child.* Rocklin, Calif.: Prima Publishing and Communication.

Wender, P. 1986. *Hyperactive Children Grown-Up.* New York: Guilford.

Wender, P. 1987. *The Hyperactive Child, Adolescent, and Adult.* New York: Oxford Press.

Wodrich, D. 1994. *What Every Parent Wants to Know: Attention Deficit Hyperactivity Disorder.* Baltimore, Md.: Brookes.

JOURNALS, MAGAZINES, AND NEWSLETTERS

Addvance (888) 238-2588.

Attention! (954) 587-3700.

Brakes: The Interactive Newsletter for Kids with ADHD (800) 825-3089.

Challenge (508) 462-0495.

Chadder (954) 587-3700.

Chadder Box (954) 587-3700.

Exceptional Children (800) 232-7323.

The ADHD Report (800) 365-7006.

INTERNET RESOURCES

www.addwarehouse.com
A site selling books and other materials associated with ADHD.

www.bmpub.com
A site selling books and other material associated with ADHD.

www.add.org
Lists of resources and support groups for individuals with ADHD and their families. Also provides information regarding the National Attention Deficit Disorder Association.

www.chadd.org/
Provides links to legal issues, fact sheets, and membership information for CH.ADD.

http://www.ed.gov
Provides resources relating to many different disabilities, including ADHD.

http://www.ericec.org
Links to the ERIC clearinghouse on disabilities and gifted education, which contains a searchable database for articles, research, and other material on numerous conditions.

http://www.familyeducation.com/home/
Homepage of the Family Education Network, which provides resources for families of children with disabilities.

www.cec.sped.org/home.htm
Links to the homepage of the Council for Exceptional Children. Provides information on workshops and conferences as well as information on many different disorders of childhood.

www.healthlaw.org
Homepage of the National Health Law Program, which provides information on legal issues and services.

www.nichcy.org/
Home page of the National Information Center on Children and Youth with Disabilities (NICHCY), which provides resources on disability-related issues to families, educators, and professions.

www.ldanatl.org
Home page of the Learning Disabilities Association of America (LDA).

www.ncld.org
Home page of the National Center for Learning Disabilities
(NCLD).

VIDEOTAPES

A Continuing Education Program on ADHD by R. Reeve, M. Spessard, R. Walker, A. Welch, J. Wright, and J. Schragg. Available through the Council for Exceptional Children, 1920 Association Drive, Reston, VA 22091. (800) 232-7323.

A.D.D. from A to Z—A Comprehensive Guide to Attention Deficit Disorder by W. Bender and P. Mclaughtin. Available through the Council for Exceptional Children, (800) 232-7323.

ADHD in Adults by R. A. Barkley. Available through Guilford Publication, Inc., 72 Spring Street, New York, NY 10012. (800) 365-7006.

All about Attention Deficit Disorder by T. Phelan. Available through ADD Warehouse, 300 N.W. 70th Avenue, Suite 102, Plantation, FL 33317. (800) 233-9273.

ADHD: What Do We Know? ADHD: What Can We Do? ADHD in the Classroom, and ADHD in Adults by R. A. Barkley. Available through Guilford Press, 72 Spring Street, New York, NY 10012. (800) 365-7006.

Educating Inattentive Children: A Guide for the Classroom by S. Goldstein. Available through the Neurology, Learning, and Behavior Center, 230 South 500 Street East, Suite 1100, Salt Lake City, UT 84102. (801) 532-1484.

Facing the Challenges of ADD by The Chesapeake Institute and the Widmeyer Group. Available through the Council for Exceptional Children, 1920 Association Drive, Reston, VA 22091. (800) 232-7323.

Help! This Kid's Driving Me Crazy by L. Adkins and H. Cady. Available through PRO-ED, 8700 Shoal Creek Boulevard, Austin, TX 78757. (512) 451-3246.

It's Just Attention Disorder: A Video Guide for Kids by S. Goldstein. Available through the Neurology, Learning, and Behavior Center, 230 South 500 Street East, Suite 1100, Salt Lake City, UT 84102. (801) 532-1484.

Jumping Johnny, Get Back to Work by M. Gordon. Available through Gordon Systems, Inc., P.O. Box 746, Dewitt, NY 13214. (315) 446-4849.

Why Won't My Child Pay Attention? by S. Goldstein. Available through the Neurology, Learning, and Behavior Center, 230 South 500 Street East, Suite 1100, Salt Lake City, UT 84102. (801) 532-1484.

ORGANIZATIONS AND SUPPORT GROUPS

Adult Attention Deficit Foundation
132 North Woodward Avenue
Birmingham, MI 48009
(810) 540-6335.

Attention Deficit Disorder Association (ADDA)
19262 Jamboree Road
Pittsburgh, PA 15234
(800) 487-2282.

Children and Adults with Attention Deficit Disorder (CHADD)
1859 North Pine Island Road, Suite 185
Plantation, FL 33322
(954) 587-3700.

Learning Disabilities Association of America (LDA)
4156 Library Road
Pittsburgh, PA 15234-1349
(412) 341-1515.

National Attention Deficit Disorder Association
9930 Johnnycake Ridge Road, Suite 3E
Mentor, OH 44060
(800) 487-2282.

National Center for Law and Learning Disabilities (NCLLD)
P. O. Box 368
Cabin John, MD 20818.

National Center for Learning Disabilities (NCLD)
381 Park Avenue South, Suite 1401
New York, N.Y. 10016
(888) 575-7373.

National Information Center for Children and Youth with Handicaps (NICHY)
P.O. Box 1492
Washington, DC 20013
(800) 999-5599.

The Council for Exceptional Children
1920 Association Drive
Reston, VA 20191-1589
(888) CEC-SPED
TTY (703) 264-9446.

The National Information Center for Children and Youth with Disabilities (NICHCY)
P. O. Box 1492
Washington, DC 20013
(800) 695-0285.

References

Achenbach, T. M. 1991. *Child Behavior Checklist, Teacher's Reporting Form.* Burlington, Vt.: Author.

Adelman, H. S., and L. Taylor. 1982. "Enhancing the Motivation and Skills Needed to Overcome Interpersonal Problems." *Learning Disability Quarterly* 5: 438–45.

Amen, D. G., J. H. Paldi, and R. A. Thisted. 1993. "Brain SPECT Imaging." *Journal of the American Academy of Child and Adolescent Psychiatry* 32: 1080–81.

American Psychiatric Association. 2000. *Diagnostic and Manual of Mental Disorders.* 4th ed. Washington, D.C.: Author.

Anastopoulos, A. D., T. L. Shelton, G. J. DuPaul, and D. C. Guevremont. 1993. "Parent Training for Attention-Deficit Hyperactivity Disorder: Its Impact on Parent Functioning." *Journal of Abnormal Child Psychology* 21: 581–96.

Barkley, R. A. 1988. "The Effects of Methylphenidate on the Interactions of Preschool ADHD Children with Their Mothers." *Journal of the American Academy of Child and Adolescent Psychiatry* 27, no. 3: 336–41.

———. 1989. "Hyperactive Girls and Boys: Stimulant Effects on Mother-Child Interactions." *Journal of Child Psychology Psychiatry* 30: 379–90.

———. 1990. *Attention Deficit Hyperactivity Disorder: A Handbook for Diagnosis and Treatment.* New York: Guilford Press.

———. 1995. *Taking Charge of ADHD: The Complete, Authoritative Guide for Parents.* New York: Guilford Press.

Barkley, R. A., G. J. DuPaul, and M. B. McMurray. 1990. "A Comprehensive Evaluation of Attention Deficit Disorder with and without Hyperactivity." *Journal of Consulting and Clinical Psychology* 58: 775–89.

Barkley, R. A., J. Karlsson, and S. Pollard. 1985. "Effects of Age on the Mother-Child Interactions of Hyperactive Children." *Journal of Abnormal Child Psychology* 13: 631–38.

Battle, J. 1992. *Culture-Free Self-Esteem Inventories—2.* Austin, Tex.: PRO-ED.

Bauermeister, J. J. 1995. "ADD and Hispanic (Puerto-Rican) Children: Some Thoughts and Research Findings." *Attention!* 2, no. 1: 16–19.

Becker, R. L., C. Schull, and K. Campbell. 1981. "Vocational Interest Evaluation of TMR Adults." *American Journal of Mental Deficiency* 85: 350–56.

Befera, M., and R. Barkley. 1985. "Hyperactive and Normal Boys and Girls: Mother-Child Interaction, Parent Psychiatric Status, and Child Psychopathology." *Journal of Child Psychology and Psychiatry* 26: 439–52.

Bender, W. N. 1997. *Understanding ADHD: A Practical Guide for Teachers and Parents.* Upper Saddle, N.J.: Merrill/Prentice Hall.

Biederman, J., R. J. Balsessarini, V. Wright, D. Knee, and J. S. Harmatz. 1989. "A Double-Blind Placebo Controlled Study of Desipramine in the Treatment of ADD: 1. Efficacy." *Journal of the American Academy of Child and Adolescent Psychiatry* 28: 7770–84.

Biederman, J., S. V. Faraone, K. Keenan, and M. T. Tsuang. 1991. "Evidence of Familial Association between Attention Deficit Disorder and Major Affective Disorders." *Archives of General Psychiatry* 48: 633–42.

Biederman, J., K. Munir, D. Knee, W. Habelow, M. Armentano, S. Autor, S. K. Hoge, and C. Waternaux. 1986. "A Family Study of Patients with Attention Deficit Disorder and Normal Controls." *Journal of Psychiatric Research* 20: 263–74.

Blackbourn, J. M. 1989. "Acquisition and Generalization of Social Skills in Elementary-Aged Children with Learning Disabilities." *Journal of Learning Disabilities* 22: 28–34.

Blechman, E. A. 1985. *Solving Child Behavior Problems at Home and at School.* Champaign, Ill.: Research Press.

Bowles, W. V., and C. G. Wirth. 1990. *Insomnia Plus . . . : The Answer to Sleeplessness.* Tulsa, Okla.: Temple Treasures.

Bracken, B. A. 1992. *Multidimensional Self-Concept Scale.* Austin, Tex.: PRO-ED.

Brown, L. L., and J. Alexander. 1991. *Self-Esteem Index.* Austin, Tex.: PRO-ED.

Callahan, M. J., and J. B. Garner. 1997. *Keys to the Workplace: Skills and Supports for People with Disabilities.* Baltimore: Brookes.

Camp, B. W., and M. A. Bash. 1985. *Think Aloud.* Champaign, Ill.: Research Press.

Campbell, D. P., and J. C. Hansen. 1981. *Strong-Campbell Interest Inventory.* Palo Alto, Calif.: Consulting Psychologists Press.

Campbell, S. B. 1990. *Behavior Problems in Preschoolers: Clinical and Developmental Issues.* New York: Guilford Press.

Center, D. B. 1989. *Curriculum and Teaching Strategies for Students with Behavioral Disorders.* Englewood Cliffs, N.J.: Prentice Hall, 1989.

Clark, L. *SOS: Help for Parents: A Practical Guide for Handling Common Everyday Behavior Problems.* Bowling Green, Ky.: Parents Press, 1985.

Conners, C. K. 1980. *Food Additives and Hyperactive Children.* New York: Plenum Press.

———. 1989. *Conners' Teacher Rating Scales.* Toronto, Canada: Multi-Health Systems.

Conners, C. K., and K. C. Wells. 1986. *Hyperkinetic Children: A Neuropsychological Approach.* Beverly Hills, Calif.: Sage.

Coopersmith, S. 1981. *Coopersmith Self-Esteem Inventories.* Palo Alto, Calif.: Consulting Psychologists Press.

Cunningham, C. E., and R. A. Barkley. 1978. "The Effects of Methylphenidate on the Mother-Child Interactions of Hyperactive Twin Boys." *Developmental Medicine and Child Neurology* 20: 634–42.

Cunningham, C. E., B. B. Benness, and L. S. Siegel. 1988. "Family Functioning, Time Allocation, and Parental Depression in the Families of Normal and ADHD Children. *Journal of Clinical Child Psychology* 17: 169–77.

DiGeronimo, T. F. 1997. *Insomnia: Fifty Essential Things to Do.* New York: Plume.

Dowdy, C. A., J. R. Patton, T. E. C. Smith, and E. A. Polloway. 1998. *Attention-Deficit/Hyperactivity Disorder in the Classroom.* Austin, Tex.: PRO-ED.

Dubey, D. R., S. G. O'Leary, and K. F. Kaufman. 1983. "Training Parents of Hyperactive Children in Child Management: A Comparative Outcome Study." *Journal of Abnormal Child Psychology* 11: 229–46.

Dunkell, S. 1994. *Goodbye Insomnia, Hello Sleep.* New York: Carol Publishing.

DuPaul, G. J. 1991. "Parent and Teacher Rating of ADHD Systems: Psychometric Properties in a Community-Based Sample." *Journal of Clinical Child Psychology* 20, no. 3: 245–53.

DuPaul, G. J., R. A. Barkley, and M. B. McMurray. 1991. "Therapeutic Effects of Medication on ADHD: Implications for School Psychologists." *School Psychology Review* 20: 203–19.

DuPaul, G. J., and G. Stoner. 1994. *ADHD in the Schools: Assessment and Intervention Strategies.* New York: Guilford Press.

Erhardt, D., and B. L. Baker. "The Effects of Behavioral Parent Training on Families with Young Hyperactive Children." *Journal of Behavior and Experimental Psychiatry* 21, no. 2 (1990): 121–32.

Erickson, M. T. 1998. *Behavior Disorders of Children and Adolescents: Assessment, Etiology, and Intervention.* 3rd ed. Upper Saddle River, N.J.: Prentice-Hall.

Fine, S., and C. Johnston. 1993. "Drug and Placebo Side Effects in Methylphenidate-Placebo Trial for Attention Deficit Hyperactivity Disorder." *Child Psychiatry and Human Development* 24: 25–30.

Fischer, M., R. A. Barkley, K. E. Fletcher, and L. Smallish. 1993. "The Stability of Dimensions of Behavior in ADHD and Normal Children over an Eight-Year Follow-Up." *Journal of Abnormal Child Psychology* 21: 337–45.

Fister, S., and K. Kemp. 1994. *Social Skills Survival Kit.* Longmont, Colo.: Sopris West.

Fitts, W. H., and G. H. Roid. 1988. *Tennessee Self-Concept Scale.* Los Angeles: Western Psychological Services.

Fletcher, J. M., B. A. Shaywitz, and S. E. Shaywitz. 1994. "Attention as a Process and as a Disorder." In *Frames of Reference for Assessment of Learning Disabilities: New Views on Measurement Issues*, ed. G. R. Lyon. Baltimore, Md.: Brookes.

Frick, P. J., B. B. Lahey, M. A. G. Chrits, R. Loeber, and S. Green. 1991. "History of Childhood Behavior Problems in Biological Relatives of Boys with Attention-Deficit Hyperactivity Disorder and Conduct Disorder." *Journal of Clinical Child Psychology* 20: 445–51.

Gilger, J. W., B. F. Pennington, and J. C. DeFries. 1992. "A Twin Study of the Etiology of Comorbidy: Attention-Deficit Hyperactivity Disorder and Dyslexia." *Journal of the American Academy of Child and Adolescent Psychiatry* 31: 343–48.

Gilliam, J. E. 1995. *Attention-Deficit/Hyperactivity Disorder Test.* Austin, Tex.: PRO-ED.

Goldstein, A. P., R. P. Sprafkin, N. J. Gershaw, and P. Klein. 1980. *Skillstreaming the Adolescent: A Structured Approach to Teaching Prosocial Skills.* Champaign, Ill.: Research Press.

Goodman, R., and J. Stevenson. 1989. "A Twin Study of Hyperactivity. 2: The Aetiological Role of Genes, Family Relationships, and Perinatal Adversity." *Journal of Child Psychology and Psychiatry* 30: 691–709.

Gresham, F. M., S. N. Elliott, and S. Evans-Fernandez. 1992. *Student Self-Concept Scale.* Circle Pines, Minn.: American Guidance Services.

Guevremont, D. 1990. "Social Skills and Peer Relationship Training." In *Attention-Deficit Hyperactivity Disorder,* ed. R. Barkley, 540–72. New York: Guilford Press.

Hallowell, E. M. 1993. "Living and Loving with Attention Deficit Disorder." *C.H.A.D.D.E.R.* 7 (special issue): 9–12.

Hallowell, E. M., and J. J. Ratey. 1994. *Driven to Distraction.* New York: Simon & Schuster.

Hamlett, K. W., D. S. Pelligrini, and C. K. Conners. 1987. "An Intervention of Executive Processes in the Problem-Solving of Attention Deficit Disorder Hyperactive Children." *Journal of Pediatric Psychology* 12: 227–40.

Hauri, P., and S. Linde. 1996. *No More Sleepless Nights.* New York: John Wiley.

Heffron, W. A., C. A. Martin, and R. J. Welsh. 1984. "Attention Deficit Disorder in Three Pairs of Monozygotic Twins: A Case Report." *Journal of the American Academy of Child and Adolescent Psychiatry* 23: 299–301.

Heffron, W. A., C. A. Martin, R. J. Welsh, and P. Perry. 1987. "Hyperactivity and Child Abuse." *Canadian Journal of Psychiatry* 32, no. 5: 384–86.

Higgins, P. 1993. *ASSIST Program.* Longmont, Colo.: Sopris West.

Hinshaw, S. P., B. N. Henker, and C. K. Whalen. 1984. "Self-Control in Hyperactive Boys in Anger-Inducing Situations: Comparative and Combined Effects." *Journal of Consulting and Clinical Psychology* 52: 739–49.

Hinshaw, S. P., B. Henker, C. K. Whalen, and D. Erhardt. 1989. "Aggressive, Prosocial, and Nonsocial Behavior in Hyperactive Boys: Dose Effects of Methylphenidate in Naturalistic Settings." *Journal of Consulting and Clinical Psychology* 5: 31–49.

Holland, J. L. 1985. *Making Vocational Choices: A Theory of Vocational Personalities and Work Environments*. Englewood Cliffs, N.J.: Prentice Hall.

Hynd, G. W., K. L. Hern, E. S. Novey, D. Eliopolus, R. Marshall, J. J. Gonzalez, and K. K. Voeller. 1993. "Attention-Deficit Hyperactivity Disorder (ADHD) and Asymmetry of the Caudate Nucleus." *Journal of Child Neurology* 8: 339–47.

Hynd, G. W., K. L. Hern, K. K. Voeller, and R. M. Marshall. 1991. "Neurobiological Basis of Attention-Deficit Hyperactivity Disorder (ADHD)." *School Psychology Review* 20: 174–86.

Jordan, D. 1992. *Attention Deficit Disorder*. Austin, Tex.: PRO-ED.

Leal, D., K. Kearney, and C. Kearney. 1995. "The World's Youngest University Graduate: Examining the Unusual Characteristics of Profoundly Gifted Children." *Gifted Child Today* 18, no. 5: 26–32, 41.

Lerner, J. W., B. Lowenthal, and S. R. Lerner. 1995. *Attention Deficit Disorders: Assessment and Teaching*. Pacific Grove, Calif.: Brooks/Cole.

Mann, C. A., J. F. Lubar, A. W. Zimmerman, C. A. Miller, and R. A. Muenchen. 1992. "Quantitative Analysis of EEG in Boys with Attention-Deficit Hyperactivity Disorder: Controlled Study with Clinical Implications." *Pediatric Neurology* 8: 30–36.

Martin, J. E., and L. H. Marshall. 1995. "ChoiceMaker: A Comprehensive Self-Determination Transition Program." *Intervention in School and Clinic* 30, no. 3: 147–56.

Mash, E. J., and C. Johnston. 1983. "Parental Perceptions of Child Behavior Problems, Parenting Self-Esteem, and Mothers' Reported Stress in Younger and Older Hyperactive and Normal Children." *Journal of Consulting and Clinical Psychology* 51: 68–99.

McBurnett, K. 1995. "The New Subtype of ADHD: Predominantly Hyperactive-Impulsive Type." *Attention!* 1, no. 3: 10–15.

McCarney, S. B. 1989. *Attention Deficit Disorder Evaluation Scale—School Version*. Columbia, Mo.: Hawthorne Educational Services.

McGee, R., F. Partridge, S. Williams, and P. A. Silva. 1991. "A Twelve-Year Follow-Up of Preschool Hyperactive Children." *Journal of the American Academy of Child and Adolescent Psychiatry* 30, no. 2: 224–32.

McGee, R., W. R. Stanton, and M. R. Sears. 1993. "Allergic Disorders and Attention Deficit Disorder in Children." *Journal of Abnormal Psychology* 21: 79–88.

Morin, C. M. 1996. *Relief from Insomnia: Getting the Sleep of Your Dreams.* New York: Doubleday.

Murphy, K. R. 1992. "Coping Strategies for ADHD Adults." *C.H.A.D.D.E.R.* 6: 10.

Nadeau, K. G. 1994. *Survival Guide for College Students with ADD or LD.* New York: Magination Press.

Naglieri, J. A., P. A. LeBuffe, and S. I. Pfeiffer. 1994. *Devereux Behavior Rating Scales—School Form.* New York: The Psychological Corporation.

Parnicky, J. J., H. Kahn, and A. B. Burdett. 1971. "Standardization of the (VISA) Vocational Interest and Sophistication Assessment Technique." *American Journal of Mental Deficiency* 75: 442–48.

Piers, E. V., and D. B. Harris. 1984. *The Piers-Harris Children's Self-Concept Scale: Revised Manual.* Los Angeles: Western Psychological Services.

Reynolds, C. R., and R. W. Kamphaus. 1992. *Behavior Assessment System for Children—Teacher Rating Scales.* Circle Pines, Minn.: American Guidance Services.

Robin, A. L. 1990. "Training Families with ADHD Adolescents." In *Attention-Deficit Hyperactivity Disorder,* ed. R. A. Barkley, 462–97. New York: Guilford Press.

Roche, A. F., R. S. Lipman, J. E. Overall, and W. Hung. 1979. "The Effects of Stimulant Medication on the Growth of Hyperkinetic Children." *Pediatrics* 63: 847–50.

Schultze, K. A., S. Rule, and M. S. Innocenti. 1989. "Coincidental Teaching: Parents Promoting Social Skills at Home." *Teaching Exceptional Children* 21, no. 2: 24–27.

Schumaker, J. B., J. S. Hazel, and C. S. Pederson. 1988. *Social Skills for Daily Living.* Circle Pines, Minn.: American Guidance Service.

Sprich-Buckminster, S., J. Biederman, S. Milberger, S. V. Faraone, and B. K. Lehman. 1993. "Are Perinatal Complications Relevant to the Manifestation of ADD? Issues of Comorbidity and Familiality." *Journal of the American Academy of Child and Adolescent Psychiatry* 32: 1032–37.

Stephens, T. M. *From Social Skills in the Classroom.* 1978. Columbus, Ohio: Cedar Press.

Strayhorn, J. M., and C. S. Weidman. "Reduction of Attention Deficit and Internalizing Symptoms in Preschoolers through Parent-Child Interaction Training." *Journal of the American Academy of Child and Adolescent Psychiatry* 28, no. 6 (1989): 888–96.

———. "Follow-up One Year after Parent-Child Interaction Training: Effects on Behavior of Preschool Children." *Journal of the American Academy of Child and Adolescent Psychiatry* 30, no. 1 (1991): 138–43.

Sue, D. W., and D. Sue. 1990. *Counseling the Culturally Different: Theory and Practice.* 2nd ed. New York: Wiley Interscience.

Ullmann, R. K., E. K. Slator, and R. Sprague. 1991. *ADD-H: Comprehensive Teacher Rating Scale.* Champaign, Ill.: MeetriTech, Inc.

Walker, H. M. 1988. *The Walker Social Skills Curriculum: The ACCEPTS Program.* Austin, Tex.: PRO-ED.

Walker, H. M., G. Colvin, and E. Ramsey. 1995. *Antisocial Behavior in Schools: Strategies and Best Practices.* Pacific Grove, Calif.: Brooks/Cole.

Webb, J. T., and D. Latimer. 1993. "ADHD and Children Who Are Gifted." *Exceptional Children* 60: 183–84.

Weiss, G., and L. Hechtman. 1986. *Hyperactive Children Grown Up: ADHD in Children, Adolescents, and Adults: Empirical Findings and Theoretical Considerations.* New York: Guilford Press.

Weiss, L. 1992. *Attention Deficit Disorder in Adults: Practical Help for Sufferers and Their Spouses.* Dallas, Tex.: Taylor.

Wender, P. H. 1987. *The Hyperactive Child, Adolescent, and Adult: Attention Deficit Disorder throughout the Life Span.* New York: Oxford University Press.

Williams, L., M. Lerner, T. Wigal, and J. Swanson. 1995. "Minority Assessment of ADD: Issues in the Development of New Assessment Techniques." *Attention!* 2, no. 1: 9–15.

Woodcock, R. W., and M. B. Johnson. 1977. *Woodcock-Johnson Psychoeducational Battery.* Itasca, Ill.: Riverside.

Zametkin, A. J., T. Nordahl, M. Gross, A. C. King, W. E. Semple, J. Rumsey, S. Hamberger, and R. M. Cohen. 1990. "Cerebral Glucose Metabolism in Adults with Hyperactivity of Childhood Onset." *New England Journal of Medicine* 323: 1361–66.

Zentall, S. 1993. "Research on the Educational Implications of Attention Deficit Hyperactivity Disorder." *Exceptional Children* 60, no. 2: 143–53.

About the Author

Robert Evert Cimera was diagnosed with ADHD-C during his master's program at Purdue University. He went on to earn a doctorate in special education at the University of Illinois at Champaign-Urbana with an emphasis in school-to-work transition and supported employment. He is an assistant professor at the University of Wisconsin at Oshkosh where he teaches preservice special educators and researches ADHD. He can be reached at robertcimera@yahoo.com.